WEBSTER'S FACTFINDER HANDBOOK

WEBSTER'S
FACTFINDER
HANDBOOK

Copyright © 1994 by
PMC Publishing Company, Inc.
118 East 28 Street
New York, New York 10016

ISBN: 1-881275-13-2

CONTENTS

CHAPTER I

THE SECRETARY

To be a valued and sought-after secretary requires much more than graduation from a recognized secretarial school. The secretary needs certain innate qualities that can be enhanced by effort and application but cannot be developed if they are not part of the personality to begin with.

Let it be said at the start that the superlative secretary can be either a woman or a man. Many of the most successful secretaries in the business world are men. Nevertheless, the vast majority of practitioners in the field are women, so this manual uses the feminine gender throughout.

Secretarial positions vary widely with the business firm and the secretary's immediate superior. Some executives expect merely a person to handle mail, telephones, and visitors and to take and transcribe dictation efficiently. Others expect a secretary to be close to an assistant, anticipating needs, making suggestions, and otherwise furthering the work of the office.

Nevertheless, all successful secretaries possess certain personal attributes and professional skills.

Personal Traits

First and foremost, perhaps, is personal integrity. A strong code of ethics is a must. The employer is entitled to unswerving loyalty. The good secretary never talks about business matters outside the office or about her superior's affairs to anyone inside or outside the office. The ability to keep secrets is a valuable asset in any sense of humor are valuable traits. Getting along with one's associates cannot help but grease the wheels of progress, and the ability to laugh at the ridiculous—even if it is oneself at times—can disarm most critics.

One's attitude and outlook on life shape all other aspects of personality. A general air of optimism makes all things seem possible and tends to transmit itself to others. Thus is generated an aura of helpfulness and cooperation. Conversely, a pessimistic viewpoint makes the task at hand seem less likely of accomplishment and more likely to infect one's coworkers with a sense of "Why try?"

The successful secretary works consciously to improve her effect on her fellows. A particularly important attribute is her voice and manner of speaking. To some extent the tone of voice is inborn; but it can be improved with attention and practice. An unattractive local or regional accent can be overcome. A harsh or nasal quality of the voice can be minimized by listening to mellifluous speakers on radio or television and emulating their diction.

Poise is another essential attribute. The good secretary needs to be "unflappable" in the face of awkward situations or difficult people. "A soft answer turneth away wrath," *Proverbs* tells us, and that is surely true in the modern world of business. Courtesy, tact, and discretion are indispensable qualities in the secretary.

Attention to matters of health and appearance is a high priority. One cannot look really well without feeling well. Health does bring a glow to the cheeks and a spring to the step. Cleanliness, of course, is preeminent. Shining hair and a faultless manicure improve anyone's appearance. Regular habits-early to bed, early to rise-help to avoid fatigue, which is a drain on good looks.

Style of dress varies with the type of establishment. Some offices stress the tailored look; others allow more latitude. Some even go so far as to permit slacks and sweaters. Nevertheless, in a working situation conservative dress will stand the secretary in good stead. Jingling bracelets and dangling earrings have no place behind an office desk.

Good work habits are essential to any field of endeavor and are not specific to the position. It should go without saying that the secretary should be punctual, accurate in her work, and intent upon the business at hand. Except in emergency, personal telephone calls should be reserved for her own time. She makes a point of remembering names-if necessary inventing mnemonic tricks to attach names to persons.

An excellent command of spoken and written English is indispensable to the successful secretary. The high school or business school graduate should have this proficiency. If you do not feel fully confident in this area, however, it would be to your advantage in moving ahead in your career to improve your skills. Adult courses and community college courses are widely available at nominal cost. Even failing that, however, much can be accomplished by wide reading-with a good dictionary nearby to check on meanings and pronunciations. Spend a little time becoming familiar with the phonetic symbols in the dictionary that enable you to pronounce the most unfamiliar word correctly.

Stenography and typing are, of course, the basic tools of the trade. Dictation at 120 words per minute is adequate for most situations. In this age of the electric typewriter and word processor, there seems almost no limit to the speed of typing that can be achieved by the determined practitioner.

Other basic tasks include processing of incoming

and outgoing mail, filing, and record-keeping. Knowledge of business arithmetic and simple bookkeeping can be helpful in carrying out these duties.

Competence may be required in placing telephone calls, including conference calls; screening callers and visitors according to the executive's wishes; arranging appointments; keeping and filing expense accounts; ordering supplies; arranging meetings; making travel reservations; writing original letters; operating office machines; doing research, and running the office in the absence of the employer. Not all of these duties may be in a particular job description, but they may well be expected of "the complete secretary."

Planning is an integral part of the secretary's day. She organizes her work, anticipates problems, and paces herself to get all accomplished with minimum wear and tear on herself and her disposition.

The modern office has many devices to facilitate the secretary's work. The electric typewriter and word processor have been mentioned. The photocopier has become a machine of many capabilities beyond merely making file copies of correspondence. It can enlarge or reduce in size; copy on both sides of the page; sort and collate; and even bind pages into pamphlets.

Some color copiers can produce reports fit for the chairman of the board or the annual meeting.

Another piece of office equipment that has become almost indispensable in a very brief span of time is the fax-or, more formally, facsimile machine. The fax sends information virtually instantaneously by telephone wire to a similar machine in another location nearby, in a distant city, or halfway around the world. It can transmit printed, typed, handwritten, or drawn material. Some units can operate with standard bond or xerographic paper. Some can be used to tape and replay spoken messages. Some can even double as copiers for internal office use.

The fax can operate manually or automatically. In manual use the operator dials the telephone number of the party wanted and asks to have the start button pressed. She then starts her machine and hangs up the telephone. In automatic operation, a preprogrammed number is pressed, and the equipment does all the rest.

So ubiquitous has the fax become that it has moved into the home even faster than has the personal computer. Faxes are now in use to place orders to mail-order merchants, to communicate with friends, and even to order pizzas at the neighborhood fast-food emporium.

CHAPTER II

THE SECRETARY'S DUTIES

Office Etiquette

In many offices the secretary is the first person a visitor encounters. The impression made at that first meeting can color an entire business relationship. The secretary's own appearance has been touched upon. Equally important is the appearance of her surroundings. It is unlikely that she will be expected to keep her office clean, but it is certainly her responsibility to keep it tidy and functional: Her desk should be shipshape at all times-no used coffee cups or cluttered ashtrays. If she herself has not overcome a smoking habit, she can do her life a favor by undertaking one of the numerous cessation programs.

Courtesy, patience, and tact are the hallmarks of the successful secretary. These attributes are exhibited in her dealings with everyone with whom she comes in contact-coworkers as well as visitors. She carries out all commitments punctually and fully.

Internal office etiquette must be learned by observation. Some offices operate with considerable informality; others maintain strict decorum. Many adopt a first-name basis between executives and employees. Better, however, to err on the side of formality. Calling a vice president "Joe" without specific invitation could lead to an early perusal of the want ads.

Gossip is to be avoided at all costs. The secretary is often privy to information about office matters-hirings, promotions, firings. Such information should remain private with-her until it has become a matter of open knowledge.

The secretary's relationship with the executive for whom she works is central to her success. She must gauge carefully what is expected of her and adhere carefully to those expectations. Some employers consider a secretary an assistant and are open to comments and suggestions. Others are offended at such a thought and want no more than prompt acquiescence to orders. In either situation, however, the employer's decisions are not open to argument.

Increasingly in today's business world the executive is a woman. The secretary should put aside any notions about its being hard to work for a woman boss. Male or female, the executive has achieved that standing by business acumen and hard work, which should be accorded the respect and deference they deserve. Forget the pejorative terms you have heard applied to women bosses: petty, catty, impossible to get along with. All of them are equally applicable to the male of the species.

A situation frequently encountered in large offices

is the necessity of working for two or more persons. It may be difficult to avoid any show of favoritism, but it is nevertheless essential. One boss may be congenial and the other hard to please, but their work should receive equal treatment from the secretary. In most cases a difference of rank will exist between the several executives, and the secretary may take her cue from that. However, the nature of a given assignment-its immediacy or lack thereof-can also be a guide as to the time preference it receives.

Use of the Telephone

The telephone is so much a part of our daily lives that it may seem gratuitous to discuss its use in the office. Handled properly, however, it can be an instrument for creating goodwill and improved business. On the other hand, poor telephone manners can lose friends and alienate people.

We have discussed the value of a pleasant speaking voice. On the phone, that voice is the whole you. The caller judges you (and sometimes your employer) by what you say, but almost as much by the way you say it. Courtesy is essential-even if you know that the caller is going to represent a major nuisance. The call may be interrupting your other work, but the telephone is a vital communication link in business and must be respected as such.

The telephone should be answered promptly. Many companies have established specific telephone greetings, which should, of course, be followed. Absent such, however, an appropriate formula is, "Mr. Doe's office." If desired, you may add, "Miss Roe speaking."

Some executives prefer to answer their own telephone. If not, most have distinct preferences as to how they are notified of calls.

It may be your duty to screen calls to avoid interrupting the executive for matters that could or should be handled by others. If so, considerable exercise of judgment is required. A caller of whom you have never heard may turn out to be an important source of information or new business for your employer or your company.

If it is necessary to transfer a call to another person, be sure not to leave the caller hanging on an unanswered line. If the person to whom you wish to transfer the call is not available, do the caller the courtesy of taking a message to that person-and delivering it!

Protocol for placing calls for the employer varies. Some executives expect the person called to be on the line before they pick up the telephone. Others consider it a matter of courtesy to be on the line first when they have initiated the call. In some situations relative rank is the determinant: The person of lower rank is on the line before the person of higher rank picks up.

Some offices maintain telephone logs of all incoming and outgoing calls. In fact, in some offices the practice is mandatory. Such information can be useful in case of billing problems. It can also be valuable in reconstructing a sequence of events at a later date. Such logs may be retained for several years.

Types of Telephone Service

Beyond the area of local calls is the vast array of telephone services available. They include station-to-station and person-to-person calls, international direct dialing, and conference calls.

When making long-distance calls, you have two options. If you are fairly sure that the person wanted will be available at the time of your call, you can place the call station to station. In that case your call will be charged by the telephone company if anyone answers at the called number. This is the most economical long-distance call.

If you wish to speak only to a specific person, you can make a station-to-station call by dialing O before the area code. This will alert an operator, who will come on the line and take the name of the person being called. You will not be connected to the number unless that person is available to take the call. The rate for person-to-person calls is somewhat higher than for station-to-station, but money is obviously saved if your call cannot be completed.

Your telephone directory is usually a source of considerable helpful information, such as area codes for major United States cities and a map showing time zones across the country.

More than one hundred countries around the world, from Algeria to Yugoslavia, can now be called by direct dialing. Of course, these calls are the equivalent of station-to-station calls in the United States: You are charged for the call if anyone answers the telephone.

To place an international call, dial 011, followed by the country and city prefixes (which are like our area codes), then the telephone number of the person or firm wanted. A list of these codes and the time difference relative to Eastern Standard Time is given on pages 204-213.

In these days of cost-consciousness in business, the conference call has assumed ever greater importance as companies seek to reduce travel expenses. A conference call can involve as many persons and locations as desired. To place such a call, dial the operator and ask for the conference operator. Give that operator the time at which you want the call placed and the names and telephone numbers of those who are to participate. At the appointed time the operator will get all parties on the line at once. Conference calls are charged as a person-to-person call to each number involved.

Visitors to the Office

Receiving visitors is an important aspect of the secretary's duties. Visitors must be greeted pleasantly and made to feel welcome, whether or not they are expected.

If you know that your employer has an appointment (and you certainly should know), and the person appears at the expected time, you can say, "Good afternoon, Mr. Roe. Mr. Doe is expecting you." People always like being addressed by name. If you are not aware that your employer has an appointment, you may ask politely, "May I ask who is calling?"

Absent an appointment, the secretary must try to ascertain the reason for the visit. She may say, "Mr. Doe is busy at the moment; could I be of help?" If that does not elicit the desired information, it may be necessary to say that you are not permitted to make appointments without knowing the subject matter.

On the other hand, you may know the visitor and therefore be obliged to decide whether your employer will want to see him if time permits. It may be a personal friend or a very important person. In such case you can either use the intercom to inform your employer or take the caller's card into the office to let him decide on his course of action.

Such an unexpected visitor may have to wait a few minutes. Either take his coat or show him where to put it. Seat him comfortably with access to reading matter, and return to your work.

If you are quite sure that the caller is someone your employer will not want to see, it is up to you to do the unpleasant chore of getting rid of him-tactfully, if possible. You can say that the executive will be busy for quite a while and suggest that the visitor write him a letter stating his business and asking for an appointment.

Announcing Visitors

If the visitor has an appointment, merely buzz your employer on the intercom, say, "Mr. Doe, Mr. Roe is here," and ask Mr. Roe to go right in.

Absent an appointment, if you are fairly sure that your employer will see the visitor, go into the office and inform him who is outside. That gives him the option of saying he is too busy, coming out and speaking to the visitor briefly to save time, or telling you to show the visitor in.

Large offices often have a central reception room staffed by a receptionist to notify individual executives that they have visitors. In such a case, if the visitor is to be escorted to the executive's office, the secretary should identify herself to the visitor: "Good afternoon, Mr. Jones, I am Miss Roe, Mr. Doe's secretary. Will you come this way?"

Desk Calendars

Most executives keep an appointment calendar on their desk. This may take one of several forms: a day at a glance, a week, or a month. When outdated, these calendars are often filed for several years as reference.

The secretary should also keep a desk calendar and keep it up-to-date with her employer's engagements as well as reminders to herself of other time commitments.

Incoming Mail

The method of handling mail depends on the size of the office. In a small office the secretary may sort and distribute the mail. A large firm usually has a central mail facility, and a given secretary is responsible only for the correspondence addressed to her immediate superior.

In the latter case, the secretary opens and sorts the mail. Whether she opens envelopes marked *Personal* or *Confidential* depends on her employer's instructions.

Envelopes should be opened carefully with a letter opener to avoid damaging enclosures. Care should be taken to remove all the contents of each. In many offices the date is stamped on each item.

The mail is sorted by type: letters and memos, bills, orders, advertisements, and publications. They are placed in that order on the executive's desk, with publications to one side.

If a letter refers to or answers a previous letter, some employers like to have such material pulled from the files and attached to the new correspondence.

Outgoing Mail

The handling of outgoing mail also depends on whether or not your company has a mail room. If mail is centrally processed, the secretary's responsibility is limited to being sure that addresses are correct and complete, that letters are properly signed and contain pertinent enclosures, and that instructions such as class of mail or special services are attached.

If the secretary stamps and mails correspondence herself, she must check the weight of each item to determine the amount of postage required and affix it carefully. If special services are called for, such as Registered Mail or Certified Mail, it is her responsibility to go to the post office and procure the necessary documentation and postage.

In today's business even many small offices invest in a postage meter. The postage meter seals envelopes and imprints them with the correct amount of postage and a dated postmark. Formerly it was necessary to take the machine to the post office periodically to have the postage replenished. Currently this can actually be done by telephone. According to postal authorities, these machines improve accuracy and save postage.

No matter who has the final responsibility for outgoing mail, the secretary should check every item before sealing the envelope. Make sure the letter is signed. If you signed it in your employer's absence, be sure to place your initials under his name. Be sure that all enclosures are in the envelope. The Postal Service discourages the use of paper clips because of the widespread use of machines in mail handling-including the postage meter. Enclosures may be stapled, if small. Otherwise fold them with or to the same size as the letter they accompany. Very small enclosures, such as business cards or coins, may be taped to the letter, or to a card or separate sheet of paper, using the type of transparent tape that lifts off with relative ease.

Like everything else done in the office, the appearance of outgoing letters is important. A badly folded letter speaks to the carelessness or indifference of the sender. Most business mail is 8 1/2 x 11 inches in size and takes a No. 10 envelope. Such letters are correctly folded in thirds. The bottom of the sheet is folded upward slightly less than one third. The top of the page is then folded down to within an eighth or a quarter of the original fold. The folded letter is then inserted in the envelope with that small margin at the bottom. In that way the letter will be right side up when removed from the envelope.

Dictation

The practice of dictation has undergone significant changes in recent years as the age of technology has progressed. Dictating machines of various types have increasingly displaced the stenographer's pad and pencil. The machines have decided advantages for both the executive and the secretary. They enable the executive to dictate at any time and place. They free the secretary to do other tasks, thus cutting in half the time involved in the dictation process.

The competent secretary is equally comfortable with either process. In the vast majority of small to mid-sized offices, however, the pad and pencil still reign supreme.

The secretary should always be prepared to report to the call of, "Take a letter." Her shorthand pad should be ready, with a rubber band holding together the filled pages, and a supply of sharpened pencils or a ball-point pen at the ready. Date each dictation session at the beginning. If you work for more than one person, put his or her initials at the end.

Be particularly careful about numbers, dates, and names in taking dictation. It is best to spell out names in longhand and to question them if there is any possibility of error.

The secretary is entitled to ask the dictator to speak more slowly. After all, accuracy is of the essence. Also, the flow of thoughts and speech when a person is intent on the subject at hand may easily outpace even the fastest stenographer.

Some secretaries like to use only the left column of the ruled page, leaving the right column blank for any changes the dictator may make or for clarification that she herself may enter when rereading the shorthand notes before transcribing them.

Your shorthand system will have its own symbols for punctuation, but you might well decide how to indicate words to be capitalized or underscored: perhaps three lines under the word for all capitals and a single line for underscoring.

Take advantage of pauses in the dictation to clarify any doubtful characters that you have written and to make mental notes of questions you might want to ask the dictator when the letter or memorandum is finished.

Transcription

It is wise, when possible, to transcribe shorthand notes immediately. Even the best notes tend to go stale if left too long.

Go over your notes before you begin to type. Be sure to verify the spelling of names and the correctness of addresses and dates. The secretary should ascertain early on how her employer feels about contributions from her to his language. Some executives welcome corrections in grammar; others have considerable pride of authorship and consider that she has overstepped herself. Be sure you know how far you may go in editing and polishing his work. Ask about anything that seems questionable.

Reading your notes before transcribing them will also enable you to estimate the length of a letter in order to position it correctly on the letterhead.

When you have finished transcribing an item, draw a vertical line through the shorthand notes.

If your employer uses mechanical dictation, you will of course familiarize yourself with operation of the machine. In other respects, however, the process is similar. Listen to a section of the material to be transcribed and decide on any grammatical corrections or editorial changes that may be indicated. Ask any questions of fact or style that may occur to you.

Many dictation machines have devices that indicate the number of words in a dictated section. This can assist you in judging placement of the material on the page.

Reminder Systems

The basic reminder system for both executive and secretary, as mentioned earlier, are their coordinated desk calendars. The secretary's calendar, however, should record more than the day's appointments and meetings.

Secretaries often start a new year by entering such other particulars of the employer's business as birthdays and anniversaries, payment dates, renewal dates, and tax dates. An even better idea is to add such reminders on a page a few days before the actual date.

Tickler files are another helpful reminder system. Tickler files take several forms. However, the file folder system is probably the most useful, since it is self-contained.

You might set up a folder for each month of the year. Then behind the folder for the current month set up a folder for each day of the month. When a matter needs follow-up, merely drop copies of the pertinent correspondence or other material into the proper folder.

Each day check the appropriate folder and deal with whatever it contains. The empty folder is then moved ahead to its position in the next month.

Filing

Despite the advance of computerization, filing of original correspondence and copies of replies is a basic part of the secretary's routine. It is imperative for her to be able to produce requested material promptly.

The principal filing systems are alphabetical, by subject, numerical, geographic, and decimal. Of these, the alphabetical system is by far the most widely used in the average office. Material is organized by name and filed alphabetically. Even when other systems are used, material within the various categories may still be alphabetized.

A subject file may be used when names are less important than the subject; for example, Insurance or Taxes.

A geographical file might be useful, for instance, to a sales organization with farflung representatives. The file might be organized by state, county, or city.

Numerical and decimal systems are highly specialized and are not likely to concern the secretary in normal business usage.

Alphabetizing

Alphabetizing can be done in one of two modes: the letter-by-letter mode or the word-by-word mode.

Letter-by-letter alphabetizing is carried throughout the entire entry, ignoring all spaces and punctuation.

Word-by-word alphabetization differs in that the principle stops with the first word. Subsequent words are considered only when two or more entries begin with the same word.

Compare the following lists:

Letter-by-Letter	Word-by-Word
Newark	New Bedford
New Bedford	New Canaan
Newbridge	New England
New Canaan	New Mexico
New England	New York
Newfoundland	New Zealand
Newmarket	Newark
New Mexico	Newbridge
New York	Newfoundland
New Zealand	Newmarket

Most style authorities insist on the letter-by-letter system. Be warned, however: Some widely used references use the word-by-word system, notably the telephone directory.

Names of people are typed on file folder labels by

surname, first name, and middle name or initial:
    Doe, John J.
    Companies named for persons are similarly indexed:
    Doe, John J. & Co.
    Otherwise firm names are alphabetized by the first word in the name:
    Bayside Medical Center
Items are alphabetized by the first word, then the second word, and so on. Articles such as *The* are placed at the end, except in foreign words:
    House of Arden, The
    Le Maison Arden
Several successive letters are treated as single words, as are abbreviations or acronyms:
    XYZ Company
    ASCAP
    UNICEF
The abbreviation *St.* is alphabetized as if spelled out:
    Saint Paul's Cathedral, not
    St. Paul's Cathedral
In names, prefixes are considered part of the name:
    De la Mare
    MacGregor
Numbers are alphabetized as if spelled out:
    Eighth Street

Titles follow names in parentheses:

Doe, John J. (Dr.)

The following list illustrates most of the foregoing rules:

Andersen, Arthur A.

Andorra, Bank of

Delaware Bay Company

DeWine, Carl

Jones Haberdashery

Jones, John G.

Jones, John Gunderson

JTC Printing

Livingston, Paul (Dr.)

St. John the Divine Cathedral

Sindbad's Restaurant

27 Wall Street

Cross-References

Some material could logically be filed under more than one name or subject. In such cases a cross-reference sheet may be placed in the file under the alternate name. This sheet should contain the name or subject, what it concerns, the date of the material, and the location of the main entry. The label might read:

Smith & Jones, Inc.

see

Barrington Builders

Bank Accounts

Secretaries are sometimes expected to supervise checking accounts maintained by the employer. In a small business, more than one account may be maintained, one for major expenditures such as rent, and perhaps a smaller one for supplies, petty cash, and other miscellany.

The secretary is also likely to be responsible for making deposits to the account at the bank and reconciling the bank statement each month.

When writing checks for your employer's signature, it is important to enter enough information on each check stub so that a bookkeeper or accountant can identify the payment and record it correctly for tax purposes.

When you have entered the information on the stub, do the necessary arithmetic immediately, so that the balance in the account can always be seen at a glance. It is a good idea to use a calculator for checkbook addition and subtraction. It saves problems with errors when reconciling the monthly statement.

Checks must be completely legible; it is good practice to make them out on the typewriter. Be sure that the date on the check agrees with that on the stub.

Use the full name of the payee, but not titles such as Mr., Mrs., or Dr.

The amount of the check is entered twice. First it is given in numerals in the blank to the right of the payee's name; for example, *$100.00*. It is then spelled out on the next line: *One hundred and no/100*.

Start both amounts as close to the left margin as possible. This makes it impossible for anyone to alter the check to increase the amount for which it was drawn; for instance, to change *$100* to *$2100*, or *One hundred* to *Two thousand one hundred*.

If you should make an error in writing a check, destroy it immediately and write *Void* across the stub. Then carry forward the former balance to the next check stub. If it becomes necessary to stop payment on a check that has already been issued, telephone the bank. Provide the name of the payee and the amount, as well as the title and number of the account and the number of the check. This must be followed by written notification to the bank.

Deposit slips also should be filled out clearly and accurately. Most offices have a rubber stamp for endorsement of checks to be deposited. Checks are endorsed on the back across the left end.

Endorsements may be of three kinds: restrictive, blank, or specific.

A *restrictive* endorsement names the bank in which the check is to be deposited.

A *blank* endorsement is merely the owner's signature. It has elements of risk, because anyone else can appropriate the check by signing his name under the first endorsement and then cashing it. The risk is minimized, however, by writing *For deposit only* before the endorsement.

A *specific* endorsement intentionally turns the check over to someone else: *Pay to the order of John Doe.* Your signature below that relinquishes your right to the check.

Each month the bank sends the depositor a statement of account, giving the opening and closing balances, a list of checks that have cleared the bank, and the checks themselves.

Usually the reverse side of the statement contains a printed form for your use in reconciling the bank's record with that of the checkbook.

Put the canceled checks in order of date and compare them with the checkbook stubs. Put a mark beside each stub entry for which you have the original check. If any check written is not included with the statement, circle the amount on the stub and make a note of its number and amount.

Also check the deposits listed in the statement against those you have made. If any do not appear, add them to the balance shown by the bank.

Total the unpaid checks and deduct the amount from the balance in the statement. Also deduct any debit memos or service charges.

When these steps have been completed, your checkbook should agree with the bank statement.

MEETINGS AND TRAVEL

The nature of business is interaction among people, and that interaction frequently involves meetings. Sometimes one person merely visits the office of another to hold a discussion, or he may summon a subordinate to his office.

Often, however, situations require face-to-face conversation among a number of people, some of whom may live and work in other locations.

When that occurs, travel may come into the picture, although the progress of modern communications increasingly makes that unnecessary, and a conference call may suffice.

Preparing for a Meeting

When it has been decided to hold a meeting, the first considerations are who will attend and where they will meet. Your employer will give you the names of the participants. It is then your responsibility to notify each. In all likelihood this will be done by telephone.

A date and time having been chosen by your employer, you will call each person to find out whether the proposed schedule is acceptable. If some participants cannot be present then, your employer will have to propose another time, and the telephone procedure is undertaken anew. When all parties have agreed to a time and place, you can note those details on your employer's desk calendar and your own.

Make a list of the participants and put it in your tickler file to remind them of the date. Depending on how far in advance the meeting is scheduled, follow up with a reminder by letter or telephone call.

Your next task is to reserve a meeting room in the city chosen. If some participants must come by air, a hotel near the airport would be a convenience. If a dinner or luncheon is involved in the plan, choose a hotel that you know can handle such events satisfactorily. Your employer may also want you to reserve rooms for those participants who will stay overnight.

It may be your responsibility to prepare the meeting room on the appointed day. (If special equipment such as a projector or an audio recorder is required, be sure to reserve it well in advance and confirm that it has been delivered.) Be sure that the seating arrangements are as requested and that the lighting and air conditioning or heating are adequate. See that there are pads and pencils, glasses, and a pitcher of water. A space must also be available for the participants to leave their coats and other articles.

If refreshments are to be served, such as coffee and pastry or soft drinks, be sure the caterer has delivered the supplies and that there is a convenient service place.

Your employer will have prepared an agenda for the meeting, which you will have typed. Make copies and send one to all participants, perhaps with the reminder of the meeting, if that is done by mail.

On the meeting day, see that your employer's place at the table is supplied with everything he might need-pad and pencils, of course, and perhaps a calendar, paper clips, and a copy of the list of participants. You may also need to supply him with material from the files concerning topics on the agenda.

During the Meeting

In an all-day meeting there are likely to be telephone calls for your employer and for some of the participants. Inquire beforehand how these should be handled-whether messages should be taken, or whether the person wanted should be called to the telephone. The usual practice is to handle your employer's calls yourself and to take messages for the others. If a call is urgent, however, type the message on a slip of paper and hand it to the person unobtrusively.

Taking and Typing the Minutes

Ascertain in advance whether you are expected to take full notes to serve as the official minutes of the meeting, or simply to summarize the proceedings for your employer and the files. Verbatim notes may be required for motions, resolutions, and any controversial discussion. If so, you might use a tape recorder to back up your shorthand notes.

It is important to record names of speakers and discussions accurately. You might prepare a seating chart in order to identify speakers. Record attendance at the beginning, and note when the meeting is called to order and when it is adjourned.

After the meeting it is advisable to type the minutes as soon as possible. Submit a rough draft to your employer for approval before typing the final copy. If your company has no specific form for minutes, these general rules may be followed:

- Center the heading-the name of the group and the type of meeting-in capitals. Below that center the date in uppercase and lowercase letters.
- In the first paragraph give the day, date, hour, place, name of presiding officer, and type of meeting. Specify if a quorum was present.
- List the names of the participants, present and absent. This may be done in two columns.

- Double-space the text, with a triple space between items of business, but single-space resolutions.

- Indent paragraphs ten spaces and resolutions fifteen spaces.

- Capitalize RESOLVED and WHEREAS, and capitalize BOARD OF DIRECTORS and CORPORATION when those words refer to the group holding the meeting.

- Spell out sums of money and follow with the figures in parentheses: *One hundred dollars ($100)*.

- Use the past tense throughout.

- Make signature lines at the end for the secretary and the chairman to sign the minutes.

- Attach appropriate reports and other documents before placing the signed minutes in the minute book.

Making Travel Arrangements

To perform this duty you must first know the company's travel policies. Some companies provide executives with company credit cards on which to charge travel expenses. Some have procedures for obtaining cash advances for the purpose.

Next you need to know your employer's preferences (*and* the company's requirements) as to type of travel and hotel accommodations and whether a rental car is wanted at all stopovers.

In our day of instant communication, travel arrangements are almost universally made by telephone. Large companies usually have a travel department to coordinate the needs of all executives. In any case, you must obtain full information in advance: travel dates, departure and arrival times, car rental needs, hotel accommodations, and preferred class of travel.

If a travel department makes the actual reservations, tickets will be delivered to the executive in ample time. If you choose to use a travel agency, the tickets will also be delivered to you. If you make the reservations yourself, the tickets will be ready for pickup at the airport or train station.

Preparing the Itinerary

Notes for the itinerary should be begun as soon as the travel plans are proposed. They should cover the places to be visited, including dates and times of departure and arrival; hotel accommodations; and proposed air or rail reservations.

Also keep an appointment schedule, showing the name, title, firm, address, and telephone number of each person to be visited; the date and time of each appointment; and notes as to whether it is a lunch or dinner meeting and the topic to be discussed.

The final itinerary should be prepared in triplicate.

The original is for your employer, one copy for your employer's family, and one copy for you.

Type an appropriate heading and then enter the pertinent information in column style. Specify whether the times shown are Eastern, Central, Mountain, or Pacific time and whether standard or daylight saving time.

   FROM: (city)
   TO: (city)
   VIA: (airline or railroad)
   DEPARTURE: (date and time)
   ACCOMMODATIONS:(flight or train number)
   CAR RENTAL: (type and location)
   HOTEL:(name, address, and checkout time)

Follow the same form if there are intermediate stops, and then work in reverse for the return trip.

CHAPTER III

USING THE ENGLISH LANGUAGE

A large part of the writing that the secretary deals with is dictated by her employer. However, she herself may be called upon to draft letters and memos, and it is her responsibility to correct any obvious errors in dictated material.

For these reasons, it is essential that the secretary have a secure command of English usage, grammar, punctuation, and spelling. Also important to the production of business letters that do credit to the company is an understanding of the rules of capitalization and word division. The following sections reflect current trends in writing style in the business world.

WORD RELATIONSHIPS

Agreement of Subject and Verb

A singular subject takes a singular verb; a plural subject requires a plural verb. When other sentence elements come between subject and verb, the agreement may not be so easy to see.

The book in which all the guests signed their names *was* on the table.

The books donated to the library by Mrs. Doe *were* on the table.

The following words are generally considered to be singular and take singular verbs: *either, neither, each, anyone, someone, everyone, anybody, somebody, nobody, everybody.*

The following words are considered plural and take plural verbs: both, few, many, several.

EITHER/OR; NEITHER/NOR

When a subject is compounded with neither/nor or either/or, the verb is singular if the two nouns are singular, and plural if the nouns are plural. If one noun is singular and the other is plural, the verb agrees with the nearest subject.

Either French or Spanish *is* a good elective.

Neither he nor his associates *support* the proposal.

COLLECTIVE NOUNS

Collective nouns such as *class, company, club, crew, jury, committee* take singular verbs when the whole is considered as a unit. They take plural verbs when members of the whole are considered separately.

The class *has* elected a president.

The jury *were* polled individually after the verdict.

AGREEMENT OF PRONOUN AND ANTECEDENT

The pronoun is singular if the antecedent is singular, and plural if the antecedent is plural.

The boy did *his* best on the test.
All the boys in the class did *their* best.
The boys and the girls did *their* best.
Neither one of the boys did *his* best.

WHICH/THAT

In everyday speech *that* and *which* are often used interchangeably, but in formal writing their use should be carefully differentiated. *That* is used to introduce a restrictive or defining clause-one that defines the noun to which it is attached and cannot be omitted without changing the meaning of the sentence.

The lake *that* is the largest of the Great Lakes is Lake Superior.

Which introduces a nonrestrictive or parenthetical clause, one that could be omitted without changing the sense of the sentence.

Lake Superior, *which* is north of Wisconsin and Michigan, is the largest of the Great Lakes.

A simple way to decide is the comma test: If the clause seems to call for commas before and after it, the word is *which*.

CAPITALIZATION

Trends in capitalization tend to change with the times, as do other matters of English usage and spelling. Currently the trend is toward more use of lowercase letters. Certain fields of activity such as publishing and scientific disciplines adopt their own rules. The secretary should follow the rules of the company or organization in which she finds herself. Lacking such rules, however, the following conventions are correct.

The abbreviations for morning and evening are set lowercase with periods but no space:

a.m.; p.m.

Capitals or small capitals (in printing) are used for B.C. and A.D.

The first word after a colon is capitalized if it begins a complete sentence.

The coach emphasized his philosophy of sports: Winning is everything.

The appendix contained several items: glossary, bibliography, and index.

Important words in the titles of books and articles are capitalized:

The Winning of the West

Gone with the Wind

Geographical divisions are capitalized:

Arctic Circle

The Pacific Rim

Geographical features are capitalized when they precede the name but typed lowercase when following the name:

Lakes Erie and Ontario

The Mississippi and Missouri rivers

Directions are capitalized when part of a name but not when they merely specify a direction.

Midwest
the Union North
eastern Long Island
The river flows south

Capitalize the names of specific streets, buildings, and so on.

Mission Street
Municipal Building
street fair
building code

Capitalize the names of organizations and groups such as political parties. Use lowercase letters for nonspecific references and for political ideologies and systems.

Socialist Party
Union Club
socialism
club dues

Capitalize divisions of government.

United States Supreme Court
the Senate
Ways and Means Committee
Department of Defense

Capitalize titles of principal government officials,

especially those of the President.

Commander-in-Chief
Secretary of State
Chancellor of the Exchequer
Prime Minister

Capitalize names of specific historical periods, but type them in lowercase letters in general references.

Middle Ages
Renaissance
twentieth century
antiquity

Capitalize religious and secular holidays. The names of the seasons are typed in lowercase letters except when personified.

Good Friday
Hanukkah
winter solstice
"Come, gentle Spring . . ."

Capitalize full names of courts. Put types of courts in lowercase letters.

Supreme Court of the U.S.
the Court (Supreme)
New York Court of Appeals
juvenile court
family court
state supreme court

Capitalize titles of legislation such as acts, treaties,

and bills. Type in lowercase letters references to pending legislation and amendments and general references to legislative matters.

   Bill of Rights

   First Amendment

   SALT Treaty

   the bill

   the pending amendment

   treaty ratification

Capitalize the formal names of branches and divisions of the military services. Type general references in lowercase letters.

   U.S. Army

   National Guard

   First Battalion

   the army

   the guard

   the battalion

Capitalize numbers when they are part of a title or part of a street address under ten.

   First Bank of Boston

   Third Precinct

   Eighty-second Congress

   One Fifth Avenue

Capitalize names of deities, religious groups and organizations, and historic councils.

   the Almighty

Vatican Council II
the Gospels
the Creation
Roman Catholic Church
church
high mass
vespers
rosary
chapel

Capitalize terms of kinship only when used before a name or when standing alone in place of a name.

I talked to Uncle George yesterday.

I called Mother on her birthday.

I forgot to call my mother.

PUNCTUATION

The purpose of punctuation is to help the reader follow the writer's thoughts through twists and turns. In speech, intonation does much of that. On the printed or typed page, however, meaning may be lost without devices to separate the phrases and clauses into groups.

Punctuation can do even more: It can lend emphasis, and it can change meanings.

The careful writer uses the various marks of punctuation to lend clarity and accuracy to the interpretation of his meaning.

The principal punctuation marks are the following, alphabetically, not in order of importance: apostrophe, brackets, colon, comma, dash, ellipses, exclamation point, hyphen, leaders, parentheses, period, question mark, quotation marks, semicolon, and virgule (commonly called slash or diagonal).

Apostrophe

With nouns, the apostrophe is used to show possession. Singular nouns form the possessive by adding the apostrophe and s. Plural nouns take only the apostrophe. This rule covers proper nouns as well, including those that end in s, with a few exceptions.

Jane's book

the river's delta

the Joneses' house

Jesus' birthplace

Moses' descendants

The apostrophe is used in contractions and to indicate where numbers are omitted.

it's (it is; but *its* as a pronoun)

two o'clock

the depression of '82

For ease of reading, the apostrophe is sometimes used in making lowercase letters plural. This was formerly the universal style with numbers and capital letters as well, but it is falling into disuse.

p's and q's
the 1990s
the three Rs
YMCAs

Brackets

Brackets are not the same as parentheses. Brackets are used within quoted material to show that the writer has made an insertion in the way of comment or explanation. They are also used frequently in technical and mathematical material.

"'Twas brillig [Carroll loved to invent words], and the slithy toves . . ."

Many typewriters do not have bracket keys. The typist can improvise by using the diagonal and underscore keys: /‾‾/

Colon

The colon may be used between two independent clauses the second of which explains the first.

The summer is fading fast: It is almost September.

In current usage, however, the clauses are often made into separate sentences, using the period.

Quotations or lists are often introduced by a colon, especially if long. The colon is also used to indicate time, in biblical references, after the salutation in letters, and in footnotes and bibliographies.

7:30 p.m.
Dear Mr. Roe:
Acts 1:3
Williams, Elsa S. *Bargello*. New York: Van Nostrand
Reinhold, 1967.

Comma

The comma is probably the most widely used of the punctuation marks, although the trend is toward lesser usage.

The comma is used to separate words in a series, to separate clauses in a compound sentence, to set off introductory words in a sentence, to set off the introduction of a quotation, and after interjections and numbers having more than four digits. Commas are placed inside of quotation marks.

Apples, oranges, and pears are good eaten raw.
The plane was canceled, so we stayed overnight.
Because the manuscript was too long, the author deleted a chapter.
Hamlet's famous soliloquy begins: "To be or not to be, . . ."
Yes, our plans are virtually complete.
Well, the committee met to discuss that yesterday.
50,792

In modified block format for letters, the comma is used after the complimentary close. In personal letters it is used after the salutation.

Cordially yours,

Dear Dad,

The comma is *not* used in the following cases:

with numbers in an address:

4230 Douglas Street

to separate short clauses in a compound sentence:

He spoke and then he sat down.

to set off a restrictive appositive:

The book *Alice in Wonderland* has a sequel, *Through the Looking Glass.*

Dash

Dashes are sometimes wrongly used in place of commas or colons. Their proper use is to set off modifiers when commas may not seem strong enough.

The effects of exercise-running, jumping, weight lifting-could be seen in his physique.

The dash may be used to indicate hesitations in speech.

Well-uh-I can't remember right now.

The dash should not be used after a colon.

Ellipses

Ellipses are dots or periods used to indicate the omission of words or sentences. Three dots, spaced, are used for words missing at the beginning or in the middle of a sentence. Four dots indicate words or sentences missing at the end of a sentence; the first dot is typed like a period following the last word, and the other three are spaced.

> Driving to Canada, we passed through Yonkers, Poughkeepsie . . . and several other cities.
> "Let us now praise famous men . . ."
> ". . . Hallowed be thy name. . . . Give us this day our daily bread."

Exclamation Point

The exclamation point is intended to emphasize or express strong feeling. It is greatly overused.

> Be careful!
> How can you say that!

In quotations, the exclamation point is placed inside the quotation marks; otherwise it goes outside the point.

> "The pot is about to boil over!" she cried.
> The cook replied coolly, "I couldn't care less"!

Hyphen

The hyphen has numerous uses in written English:
To break words at the end of a line:
> ridic-ulous

To link words in a compound adjective:
> well-built houses

one- and two-page entries
To connect certain compound nouns:
self-esteem
Senator-elect
To indicate inclusive numbers:
pages 130-37
To clarify meaning when adding a prefix forms a different word:
re-cover
co-op
Compound adjectives containing an adverb ending in *-ly* do not take the hyphen:
suddenly busy secretary
fully dressed capon

Leaders
Leaders are a row of periods used to link typed items across a space. They are sometimes used in tables, indexes, and other tabular material, although their use is declining.

Preface iv
Accounts Receivable $900,000

Parentheses
Parentheses are used to set off certain elements from the rest of the sentence. Be sure to keep punctuation where it belongs, within or outside the parentheses.

The parts of a sentence are: (1) subject; (2) predicate; and (3) object.

Thirty-nine cents (39¢) .

The use of dictionaries has already been discussed (see Chapter 6).

The Occupational Directory (OD) is a valuable reference tool.

Period

The period is used to end a declarative or imperative sentence.

The player's next move produced checkmate.

Periods are also used in abbreviations, following the numbers in lists, and as decimals.

42nd St.

i.e.

The proctor's instructions were:

1. Don't talk.
2. Don't leave the room.
3. Don't cheat.

Periods are placed inside quotation marks.

"Twopence a week, and jam every other day."

Periods are not used in a vertical list unless one of the items is a complete sentence.

Periods are not used in initials of agencies, short forms of words, or Roman numerals except in lists.

OPEC
memo
George III
Chapter I.
Chapter II.

Question Mark

Sometimes called interrogation point, the question mark denotes a query or expresses doubt.

When is the first meeting?
Frederick Barbarossa (1123?-90) became Holy Roman Emperor in 1152.

A request couched as a question does not take the question mark.

Will you please deal the cards.

The question mark is placed inside parentheses, brackets, or quotation marks only when it is part of the enclosed material.

Why did he say, "I do not choose to run"?
The teacher asked, "How many have finished the test?"

Quotation Marks

Quotation marks enclose someone else's words.

"This week," he said, "we shall take up the fall of Rome."

Quotation marks also are used to enclose the titles

of magazine articles, television programs, radio programs, songs, and nicknames.

"The Discovery of Antarctica"

"The Cosby Show"

"Symphony Hall"

"Oh, Susanna"

Edward V. "Eddie" Rickenbacker

Colons and semicolons are placed outside quotation marks; periods and commas are placed inside.

Single quotation marks are used to enclose a quotation within a quotation.

"It must sometime come to 'jam today', Alice objected.

Semicolon

The semicolon may be used instead of a period between two independent clauses that are closely related.

It's your deal; I dealt the last hand.

Items in a series that has internal punctuation can be separated by semicolons.

The itinerary included stops in Hoboken, New Jersey; Dover, Delaware, and Baltimore, Maryland, before arrival in the capital.

The semicolon is placed *outside* quotations or parentheses.

Virgule

The virgule (also called *slash or diagonal*) is a slanting line used to indicate a choice between two alternatives.

and/or

in/out

It is sometimes used as a dividing line in dates and fractions.

2/22/92

2/10

The virgule may also be used to indicate the end of a line of poetry.

"I doubt it," said the Carpenter. / And shed a bitter tear."

Division of Words

Ideally, words are not divided across lines. If it is necessary, however, it is best to divide between syllables.

Words of two syllables may be divided at the end of the first syllable.

con-vent

gen-der

In words beginning with prefixes, try to divide at the prefix.

mis-construe

dis-engage

trans-fer

In words ending with suffixes, try to divide at the suffix.

agree-able

hop-ing

fin-est

Most words having double consonants may be divided between the consonants unless the stem ends in a double consonant.

forgot-ten

embar-rass

call-ing

pass-able

Compound nouns are usually divided between the two parts.

door-keeper

book-ends

type-writer

In words in which two vowels fall together but are pronounced separately, divide between the vowels.

tri-angle

pre-eminent

The following suffixes are usually good places for word division: *able, ance, ant, ence, ent, ible, ical, tive.*

compar-able

accord-ance

ten-ant

differ-ence

compon-ent
convert-ible
ident-ical
invent-ive

The list of *don'ts* in word division is longer than the *do's*.

Do not divide words of one syllable.

frieze
tripped
launch
skilled

Do not divide four-letter words.

item
lazy
opus

Do not divide a word on a single letter.

able, *not* a-ble
omit, *not* o-mit

Most suffixes should not be divided: *cial, cion, cious, geous, gious, sion, tial, tion, tious.*

gla-cial
suspi-cion
gra-cious
advanta-geous
ambi-tious
reli-gious

ascen-sion
nup-tial
voca-tion

In general, avoid dividing names of persons or other proper nouns.

Do not separate titles from the names to which they belong.

Do not separate abbreviations such as YMCA, UNICEF.

Do not separate initials from names.

Try to avoid dividing a word at the end of a paragraph or a page.

Do not permit more than two consecutive lines to end in hyphens.

As always, when in doubt look it up!

SPELLING

It is often said that some people can spell and others can't. This is a truism that is not true. Spelling correctly requires attention, careful pronunciation, and frequent resort to a good dictionary. The secretary should have within reach a desk-size dictionary, even if an unabridged version is available in the office.

Two excellent volumes are *Webster's New Collegiate Dictionary* and the *Random House Webster's College Dictionary*. Both desk references are based on their respective unabridged editions.

USING THE ENGLISH LANGUAGE

Those who find spelling troublesome can follow a few simple routines to improve their ability:

1. Learn to spell by syllables. Errors in spelling are often the result of mispronunciation.

2. Keep a list of your spelling errors and study them frequently.

3. Learn the most commonly misspelled words in the list on pages 73-74.

4. Learn the basic spelling rules that follow.

5. When in doubt, look it up.

Forming Plurals

Most nouns form the plural by adding *s*: book, books; chair, chairs.

Nouns ending in *s*, *x*, *ch*, or *sh* form the plural by adding es:

    class, classes
    box, boxes
    church, churches
    dish, dishes

Exception: Some nouns ending in *f* or *fe* change the final letters to *v* and add *es*:

    wife, wives
    sheaf, sheaves

Words ending in a consonant and *y* form the plural by changing the *y* to *i* and adding *es*:

berry, berries
cooky, cookies

Words ending in a vowel and *o* form the plural by adding *s:*

video, videos
folio, folios

Words ending in a consonant and *o* form the plural by adding *es:*

hero, heroes
tomato, tomatoes

Exception: Musical terms ending in *o* merely add *s:*

piano, pianos
contralto, contraltos

Compound nouns set as one word add *s* at the end:

cupful, cupfuls
pocketful, pocketfuls

Compound nouns set as two words or hyphenated base the plural form on the main word:

sister-in-law; sisters-in-law
trade union, trade unions

When both words in a compound noun are of equal importance, both are made plural:

woman representative; women representatives
head of department, heads of departments.

The plural of some words is formed by a change in the vowel or a complete change of spelling:

man, men

foot, feet
child, children

Proper nouns are made plural by adding *s* or-if the name ends in *s*-by adding *es:*

Jane, Janes
Jess, Jesses
Jones, Joneses

Prefixes

The principal prefixes are *in, em, im, em, dis, mis, be, re, de, il,* and *over.* The spelling of a word is not changed when one of these prefixed is added:

inexpert
enfold
impartial
employ
unnatural
disenchant
misspell
beribbon
retrace
deemphasize
illicit
overbearing

A few words add a hyphen with a prefix:

anti-American
self-esteem

Since there is no comprehensive rule governing the situation, it is wise to depend on the dictionary for guidance.

Suffixes

In words ending in silent *e*, drop the *e* when a suffix begins with a vowel:

decide, deciding

use, usage

In words ending in silent *e*, retain the *e* when a suffix begins with a consonant: manage, management

care, carefully

When adding *ed* or *ing*, the pronunciation of the base word may serve as a guide. Most words that end in a single consonant (except *f, h, x*) preceded by a vowel double the final consonant if the word is accented on the last syllable:

plan, planned, planning

extol, extolled, extolling

When the word is not accented on the last syllable, the consonant is usually not doubled:

travel, traveled, traveler

exit, exited, exiting

When the suffix *ness* or *ly* is added to words not ending in *y*, the base word is usually unchanged. In most words ending in *y*, the *y* is changed to *i* when *ly* is added:

literal, literally
similar, similarly
genuine, genuineness
happy, happily, happiness
cloudy, cloudiness

When the suffix *ness* is added to a word ending in *n*, the final *n* is doubled:

sudden, suddenness
mean, meanness

Words ending in silent *e* and preceded by *c* or *g* usually retain the *e* before the suffixes *able* and *ous:*

manage, manageable
outrage, outrageous

Only one English word ends in *sede:* supersede. Only three end in *ceed:* exceed, proceed, and succeed. All others take the ending *cede:* precede, concede.

ie/ei

After *c*, when the sound is long *e*, the *e* usually precedes the *i:*

receive
ceiling

After most other letters, the *i* precedes the *e:*

thief
believe
shield

When the sound is not long *e*, or when the sound is long *a*, the *e* precedes the *i*:

sleigh

veil

eight.

Remember the rhyme: Use *i* before *e* except after *c* or when sounded like *a* as in n*ei*ghbor and w*ei*gh.

POSSESSIVES

The possessive is usually formed by adding '*s*:

Jane, Jane's.

Use no apostrophe with possessive or relative pronouns:

his, hers, ours, yours, theirs, whose.

Use the apostrophe with singular or plural nouns ending in *s*:

hostess, hostess'

duchess, duchesses'

princes' (plural).

It is important not to confuse the possessive form with contractions:

it's (it is); its

they're (they are); their

FREQUENTLY MISSPELLED WORDS

In addition to your personal list of spelling buga-boos suggested above, spend a little time with the following words that have turned up most often on lists of frequent errors by students at various levels and by persons taking Civil Service examinations:

absence	February
accidentally	grammar
accommodate	grievance
acknowledgment	height
advantageous	hypocrisy
all right	indispensable
athletic	interested
benefited	judgment
calendar	knowledgeable
cemetery	laboratory
changeable	latter
coolly	maintenance
{ council	mischievous
{ counsel	negligible
{ desert	noticeable
{ dessert	occasion
dilemma	occurrence
embarrassed	omitted
exercise	parallel
existence	practically

{principal
{principle
 privilege
 promissory
 pronunciation
{quiet
{quite
 recommend
 referred
 relieve
 rhythm
 seize

 separate
{stationary
{stationery
 supervisor
 transferred
 relevant
 villain
 Wednesday
 weird
{woman
{women

WORDS FREQUENTLY CONFUSED

Many words are similar in sound but quite different in meaning. Others are different in both sound and spelling but are confused with each other. The following are some of the most troublesome.

accept, except *Accept* means to receive or agree to: to *accept* an invitation. *Except*, as a verb, means to take out or leave out: to *except* no one from the rules.

addition, edition *Addition* means the process of joining together or finding the sum of. *Edition* refers to the form in which a book or other publication is published: first *edition*.

advice, advise *Advice* is the noun: to give *advice*. *Advise* is the verb: to *advise* a person.

affect, effect *Affect*, as a verb, means to influence: Fear *affects* the mind. *Effect*, as a verb, means to bring about or cause: It is time to *effect* some changes; as a noun, it means the result or outcome: The *effect* of the change was gratifying.

all right, alright *All right* means allowable. It is *all right* to do so. *Alright* is not an acceptable spelling.

allude, elude *Allude* means to make indirect reference: He *alluded* to the earlier quotation. *Elude* means to avoid or escape: The suspect *eluded* capture.

already, all ready *Already* means by the time mentioned: The ship has *already* sailed. *All ready* means fully prepared: We are *all ready* to go.

among, between *Among* means in the midst of several things or persons: Settle it *among* you. *Between* refers to only two persons or things: *Between* you and me.

appraise, apprise *Appraise* means to make an evaluation of: The jeweler *appraised* the ring. *Apprise* means to notify or inform: He was *apprised* of the visitor's arrival.

ascent, assent *Ascent* means rising or climbing: The bird's *ascent* was swift. *Assent* means agreement, consent, permission: *assent* to a course of action.

between *See* among.

can, may *Can* expresses ability to do: You *can* do better than that. *May* expresses permission: You *may* attend the dance.

capital, capitol *Capital* means the official seat of government: Washington is the *capital* of the United States. *Capitol* is a building in which a legislature meets: the U.S. *capitol* is in Washington.

censor, censure *Censor* as a noun means an official examiner of literary works; as a verb it means to delete, suppress: The *censor* examined the library and *censored* a number of books. *Censure* as a verb means to express disapproval of; as a noun it means the expression of disapproval: The judge's *censure* of the defendant was stern; he *censured* both his behavior and his language.

census, senses *Census* means an official count of the population: The 1990 *Census* resulted in redistricting of the states. *Senses* (the plural of sense) means awareness or sanity: He has taken leave of his *senses*.

cite, sight, site *Cite* means to mention: to *cite* a fact. *Sight* as a noun means a view, a vision: a beautiful *sight*. *Site* means a place or location: the *site* of the school.

complement, compliment *Complement* as a noun means a part that completes another part: The feather really *complements* her hat. *Compliment* as a noun means praise, commendation: His gaze was an obvious *compliment* to her.

council, counsel, consul *Council* as a noun means an assembly for consultation: The Security *Council* decided the matter. *Counsel* as a noun means guidance, advice, or a lawyer: Her mother's *counsel* guided her well. *Counsel* for the defense opened his case. *Consul* means an official living in a foreign country to protect the interests of his own country.

creditable, credible *Creditable* means worthy of praise or esteem: His performance on the test was quite *creditable*. *Credible* means worthy of being believed, reliable: He offered a *credible* alibi.

decent, descent, dissent *Decent* means proper, respectable: He waited a *decent* interval. *Descent* means going downward: *descent* of the lighted ball at New Year's. *Dissent* as a noun means disagreement; as a verb, to disagree: He registered a strong *dissent* against the ruling.

device, devise A *device* is something invented or thought up: left to my own *devices*. *Devise* means to invent or contrive: *devise* a plan to get free.

dissent *See* decent.

edition *See* addition.

effective, effectual *Effective* means producing the desired result: The inoculation was *effective* in preventing rabies. *Effectual* means having the ability to produce a desired result: *Effectual* legal steps brought about his release.

elicit, illicit *Elicit* means to bring forth: Careful questioning *elicited* the truth. *Illicit* means illegal or unlawful: An *illicit* shipment of drugs was confiscated.

elude *See* allude.

eminent, imminent *Eminent* means high in stature, distinguished: an *eminent* statesman. *Imminent* means about to happen: in *imminent* danger.

except *See* accept.

formally, formerly *Formally* means with formality: to be introduced *formally*. *Formerly* means at an earlier time: He was *formerly* a soldier.

illicit *See* elicit.

lay, lie *Lay* means to put or place: Please *lay* the book on the desk. *Lay* is also the past tense of *lie*: *lie* down after lunch. *Lie* as a verb means to be in or to take a horizontal position: I *lie* down when I am tired.

learn, teach *Learn* means to acquire knowledge: She must *learn* her lessons. *Teach* means to impart or give knowledge: Her mother will *teach* her to read.

lessen, lesson *Lessen* means to make less, to reduce: A joke will *lessen* the tension. *Lesson* means something to be learned: The teacher assigned the third *lesson*.

loose, lose *Loose* means not fastened: The dog was *loose* in the yard. *Lose* means to mislay or be deprived of: to *lose* one's belongings.

may *See* can.

passed, past *Passed* (the past tense of the verb *to pass*) means went beyond: The sprinter *passed* me easily. *Past* as an adjective means ended, finished: The time for tears is *past*; as a noun it refers to time gone by: I keep remembering the *past*.

militate, mitigate *Militate* means to have a heavy effect: A prison record *militates* against him. *Mitigate* means to lessen in force, to make less severe: The breeze *mitigated* the heat of the day.

persecute, prosecute *Persecute* means to mistreat or harass: The Nazis *persecuted* the Jews in Germany. *Prosecute* means to bring legal action against: The district attorney will *prosecute* the case.

personal, personnel *Personal* pertains to a person: She took her *personal* effects with her. *Personnel* refers to a body of employees: The *personnel* worked on staggered shifts.

practicable, practical *Practicable* means possible of doing, usable: He proposed a *practicable* solution to the problem. *Practical* means pertaining to actual use or action: The manual gave *practical* instructions for assembling the model.

prosecute *See* persecute.

senses *See* census.

sight *See* cite.

site *See* cite.

stationary, stationery *Stationary* means remaining in one place: The diner is a *stationary* eating place. *Stationery* means writing supplies.

suite, sweet *Suite* means a set of things meant to be used together: a *suite* of furniture. *Sweet* means having a taste like sugar.

teach *See* learn

TYPING TIPS

Making Special Characters

Typewriters contain a number of special characters, but not all typewriters have all the characters a secretary is called upon to use. Many of these can be improvised by overtyping various standard letters and symbols; that is, by typing a character, backspacing, and typing another on top of the first. These will not be perfect, but they will suffice for most nontechnical purposes.

To make a paragraph mark: Overtype a capital P with a lowercase 1 (℗).

To make a division mark, combine a colon and a hyphen: (÷).

To make an exclamation mark, type an apostrophe over a period (!)

To make a degree mark, turn the platen slightly toward you and type a lowercase o: (°).

To make brackets, use the diagonal and underscore keys (/‾ ‾/).

To make a section sign, type one lowercase s over another, with the second slightly raised (§).

To make an equals mark, type two hyphens, the second slightly above the first: (=).

To make a cedilla, type a lowercase c and a comma underneath it: (ç).

To make a caret, use the underscore and the diagonal (_/).

To make a plus sign, type a hyphen and a diagonal on top of it: (∤)

To make a pound sterling sign, type a capital L and a hyphen: (Ł).

To make the signs for minutes and seconds (or inches and feet), type an apostrophe (') and quotation marks (").

Typing on Forms and Ruled Lines

Forms seldom seem designed to fit the typewriter on which they are being filled out. To avoid a sloppy appearance, follow these procedures:

Adjust the form in your machine so that the letters strike slightly above the ruled lines, preferably so that the tails of letters *g, p, q* and *y* just touch the line. It is quite possible that the line spacing will be different from that of your typewriter; if so, adjust for the difference by using the variable line spacer. It will mean forwarding the platen by hand, but it will yield a neatly typed form.

If the form includes boxes to be checked, it may be necessary to shift the paper slightly to the right or left at the beginning of the task, so that the x falls squarely in the boxes.

Typing Numbers and Fractions

The average secretary has relatively little need to type numbers and fractions, but a few simple rules will cover most situations that you might encounter.

Some typewriters have keys for one half and one quarter. These are fine to use if no other fraction occurs in a particular typing job. All fractions in a given document should be typed in the same style, however (1/8, 2/5, 3/10, 1/2, 1/4).

In typing mixed fractions, leave a space between the whole number and the fraction: 2 1/2.

Numbers that occur in textual material may be handled in one of two ways, depending on your employer's preference:

Numbers ten and below are spelled out; all others are in figures.

Or, numbers one hundred and below, and larger round numbers such as two thousand, are spelled out; all others are in figures.

In either case, if you use a large number (such as 125) within a given paragraph, all other numbers in that paragraph should be typed in figures, including ten and below.

When typing numbers in columns, align them by a sign that they have in common, such as decimals, dollar signs, or percent marks. If there are more than a few, you can set tabular stops to make it easier.

If figures have nothing in common, type them either flush left or centered.

5%	5 percent
$70	seventy dollars
200 lb.	200 pounds

Do not divide numbers at the end of a line of text.

Making Corrections

Some copy is required to be perfect. Certain legal documents, for instance, may not have erasures or other corrections.

In practical usage, however, meticulously made deletions and corrections may be acceptable.

If in typing you notice an error while the page is still in the typewriter, it can be carefully erased or covered by correction fluid and retyped correctly.

If the page has been removed from the typewriter,

however, it must be realigned to permit retyping after the error has keen eliminated. This is best done by finding a capital I or T near the correction to line up with. Failing that, the next best is a lowercase i, using the dot as guide.

Modern typewriters have built-in correction devices that lift the incorrect letters off the page and permit almost undetectable correction.

Correction fluid is painted with a tiny brush over the error. When it is dry, a relatively neat correction can be made by typing over it. Correction fluid is available in a wide assortment of colors to match your paper stock.

Spacing and Punctuation Marks

The rules for spacing after punctuation marks are principally a matter of long usage, but they are widely accepted in business and should be observed by the careful secretary.

The basic rule is that punctuation is not separated from the word it follows. For instance, a dash that follows the word at the end of a line must be on that line, not the succeeding line.

Leave *no* space in the following situations:

• Between a word and the punctuation that follows it:

    to the end;

- Before or after a dash:
  Early-at seven p.m.
- Between quotation marks and the quoted matter:
  "Jane Eyre" is a great novel.
- Before or after a hyphen:
  twenty-six
- Before or after an apostrophe:
  Henry's
  where's
- Between items separated by a virgule (diagonal):
  Day/Glo
  and/or
- Between the initials of an abbreviation:
  p.m.
- Between parentheses or brackets and the words they enclose:
  Seventh (and last) is . . .

Leave *one* space:

- After a comma:
  . . . now, and so forth
- After a semicolon:
  (2) keep it short; and (3) . . .
- After a period following an initial or in an abbreviation:
  John R. Doe

Roe Printing, Inc. is our supplier.
- After a suspended hyphen:
  the first- and second-grade classes.
- Before and after x when standing for *by:*
  9 x 12.

  Leave *two* spaces:
- After punctuation ending a sentence:
  . . . it was gone! I couldn't find it anywhere.
- After a figure or letter introducing an item in a list:
  1. Long division
       a. Dividend and divisor

CHAPTER IV

BUSINESS LETTERS

The business letter is a representative of the writer and the company that employs him or her. The content of the letter is largely out of the purview of the writer's secretary; so is the quality and design of the letterhead on which it is typed. Just about everything else about it, however, is the responsibility of the secretary.

The format of the business letter may be established by company policy. If so, of course, the secretary follows it. If not, however, the secretary has considerable latitude in establishing that format.

In the days of handwritten letters, paragraph indention was used for purposes of clarity. The advent of the typewriter put an end to that, and current usage almost universally has adopted either the full block form or the modified block form.

Full Block Form

The full block form is popular in many offices because of its simplicity and air of modernity. Everything under the letterhead-date, address, salutation, body of letter, complimentary close, and signature-is aligned at the left margin, or, as is said in printing, flush left.

Full Block Form

February 6, 1992

Mr. John Doe
John Doe Publishers, Inc.
1234 West 23rd Street
New York, NY 10001

Dear Mr. Doe:
It was a pleasure to meet you yesterday . . .
and I hope to see you when I am in the city again.

Sincerely yours,

Richard Roe
Vice President

Modified Block Form

The modified block form is probably the most widely used in current business practice. In this form the principal elements of the letter are typed flush left, but certain parts-the date, the complimentary close, and the signature-are aligned at the right margin to give a sense of balance to the page.

Modified Block Form

February 24, 1992

Mr. John Doe
John Doe Publishers, Inc.
1234 West 23rd Street
New York, NY 10001

Dear Mr. Doe:
It was a pleasure to meet you yesterday . . .
and I hope to see you when I am in the city again.

Sincerely yours,

Richard Roe
Vice President

Some companies utilize the full block form for short letters, in which it has a more pleasing effect, and the modified form for longer letters.

Semiblock Form

This is a more traditional format. It differs from the modified block only in that paragraphs are indented five to ten spaces.

Official Style

This format is used for official communications, as with members of government or the armed forces. It is also used for personal letters written on special, smaller, company stationery.

The dateline and salutation are placed as in the modified block form. The address, however, is typed flush left two to five lines below the signature. Paragraphs are indented two to ten spaces.

PARTS OF LETTER

Placement

Regardless of format chosen, it is essential that the letter be so placed as to create a pleasing appearance. The body of the letter should be centered in the page, with ample margins to left and right.

Punctuation

The modern trend is to eliminate unnecessary punctuation in all writing. This is also true in business letters.

Especially when using the full block format, secretaries usually choose open punctuation. In this style, punctuation is used only in abbreviations. None is used in the salutation or complimentary close.

Mr. John Doe
John Doe Publishers, Inc.
1234 West 23rd Street
New York, NY 10001

Dear Mr. Doe

Sincerely yours

Many secretaries modify the open style by using punctuation for the salutation and complimentary close.

Mr. John Doe

John Doe Publishers, Inc.
1234 West 23rd Street
New York, NY 10001

Dear Mr. Doe:

Sincerely yours,

Dateline

The dateline customarily gives month, day, and year:

February 6, 1992

Some stylists prefer the form used by the military and in Great Britain: day, month, and year:

6 February 1992

In full block format, the dateline is typed flush left, two to four inches below the letterhead. In modified style is it placed flush right at the margin of the letter. Some secretaries like to vary the style by centering the dateline under the letterhead.

In any case, the month is spelled out, not abbreviated, nor are the suffixes *-st, -nd,*
-rd, or *-th* used in the day of the month:

February 6, not Feb. 6th.

Inside Address

The inside address consists of the name of the person addressed, the name of the firm if applicable, the street address, and the city, state, and zip code. If the person is addressed at a place of business, his or her title is placed after the name or on a separate line. The title is never abbreviated. The full corporate title of the company is always used; this can be found on the company's letterhead or billhead. Carry-over lines of the address are indented about three spaces.

Only courtesy titles and professional titles precede the name of the addressee: Mr., Mrs., Miss, Ms., and Professor or the Reverend. If a professional degree follows the name, the title is omitted before it:

Dr. John Doe, *but*

John Doe, M.D.

Some stress has been laid on the avoidance of abbreviations. There is one exception, however: The official Postal Service abbreviations should be used in all addresses. These are given on pages 146-148.

With the advance of technology, the five-digit zip code-which took so long to be universally accepted-has now been lengthened by four digits. This addition is currently being phased in and is used principally by large mailers. The alert secretary would be well advised, however, to keep an eye out for the nine-digit code on mail that passes through her hands and make a note of it in addresses that are frequently used in her office. As machines are increasingly pressed into use in the Postal Service, it will become as essential a part of the business address as the "old-fashioned" five-digit code.

Salutation

In business correspondence, salutations are usually formal: Dear Mr. Doe; Dear Dr. Doe; Dear Mrs. Roe; Dear Ms. Roe. If there is a relation of friendship between the writer and the addressee, it is permissible to use first names: Dear John; Dear Mary. If the name of the person addressed is not known, one may write Dear Sir or Dear Madam. If no individual is intended, the salutation may be Gentlemen or Ladies.

Special forms of address are used for government officials and members of the armed forces, the church, and the professions. These are given beginning on page 108.

Body of Letter

The body of the letter is, of course, the heart of the letter. Its quality and effectiveness will depend on the skill of the dictator or writer.

The competent secretary can nevertheless make a difference by ensuring that the letter is visually appealing. Many dictators specify paragraphs. If that is not done, however, paragraphs should be of moderate length and, if possible, be confined to a single idea.

The body of the letter is single-spaced unless it

consists of only a few lines. Double-spacing is used between paragraphs.

References to newspapers, periodicals, books, paintings and sculptures, operas, and long musical compositions are underlined to indicate italic type. References to motion pictures, television and radio programs, and articles in periodicals are placed in quotation marks.

Complimentary Close

The complimentary close takes its tone largely from the salutation and the degree of formality or intimacy shown in that part of the letter. A letter that opens with Dear Sir or Dear Madam would appropriately close with Yours truly, Yours very truly, or Very truly yours.

A letter that opens with Dear Mr. Doe or Dear Ms. Roe might close with Yours sincerely, Very sincerely yours, or even Cordially yours, depending on the degree of friendliness evidenced in the body of the letter.

Letters between friends, of course, may close with an expression of that friendship, such as Regards, or Best regards.

Signature

The signature consists of the name of the writer and his or her position in the firm. If the writer is an officer of the company and his or her name appears in the letterhead, it is not necessary to type the name under the signature.

A four-line space is left for the written signature.

If the company name is part of the signature, it is usually capitalized. The name of the person signing is typed below the actual signature, in uppercase and lowercase letters. A title follows the name on the same line or a separate line.

JOHN DOE PUBLISHERS, INC.

Richard Roe
Vice President

The tendency among women in business is to drop the titles Mrs., Miss, or Ms. in title lines. In some cases, however, married women prefer to use the title to make it easier for correspondents to address them correctly. It is usually typed:

(Mrs.) Jane Doe

and signed:

Jane Doe

Certain additional information is provided in some business letters but not in all. This includes the attention line, the identification line, the enclosure line, the carbon copy line, and the postscript.

Attention Line

This line is used when a letter is addressed to a firm but is intended for the attention of a particular person. Its use indicates that the letter may be opened by others if the person identified is not available.

The attention line appears on both the envelope and the letter. On the envelope it is typed either as the second line of the address, or below and to the left of the address.

In the letter it is typed two spaces below the address and two spaces above the salutation. In a full block form letter the attention line is flush left. In modified or semiblock it is centered on the page.

Attention: John Doe

Since such a letter is addressed to a firm, the salutation is impersonal:

Gentlemen:
Dear Sirs:
Ladies:
Mesdames:

Identification Line

This information is placed flush left one or two lines below the signature. It usually consists of the initials or the full name of the writer and the initials of the secretary, separated by a colon.

JD:jr
John Doe: jr

Enclosure Line

This line notifies the recipient (and reminds the secretary) that additional material has been enclosed with the letter. It is typed flush left directly below the identification line. Several styles are employed:

Enclosure
Enc.
Enc (2)
Enclosure: Check $750.75
            Return envelope
            Policy #9876-5432

Carbon Copy

This term is still commonly used although carbon paper is not, having largely given way to photocopying. When a copy is to be sent to a person other than the addressee, the fact is indicated in the business letter, just below the identification line.

John Doe: jr
cc: Jane Roe

In a situation in which it is not desired for the addressee to know of the copy, the information is placed only on the office copy of the letter. Called a blind copy, it is then indicated thus:

bc: Jane Roe

Postscript

Postscripts are seldom used in business letters, being considered evidence of sloppy thinking and failure to marshal thoughts on the writer's part. At times, however, the postscript is used deliberately as a method of attracting attention or emphasizing a point in the body of the letter. The postscript is placed two or three lines below the identification line, and preceded by the letters P.S. and a colon.

The Envelope

The appearance of the envelope should match the letter it encloses in style and attractiveness of presentation. The address is usually typed single-spaced and in block form. It is placed slightly to the left and just below the center of the envelope.

If the firm name is imprinted in the upper left corner, the writer's name may be typed above it.

It is advisable to use the Postal Service official two-letter abbreviations for the names of states. It is essential to use the zip code, including the new four-digit addition, if available. No characters of any kind should follow the zip code; they may interfere with the automatic scanning machine.

Notations and directions are handled variously. Attention lines are usually typed at the bottom left of the envelope. Notations such as *Personal, Confidential*, or *Hold for Arrival* are customarily placed above and to the left of the address.

Instructions regarding type of postal service, such

as Registered, Certified, and Special Delivery, are typed at the upper right, just below the space for postage stamps or postage meter imprint.

THE MEMORANDUM

This format is used principally for internal use, but it is sometimes utilized for external communications. Most firms have special stationery for memorandums. It is usually of less expensive paper stock and printed instead of engraved.

Some memo stationery has preprinted headings such as the following:

    Date:
    To:
    From:
    Subject *or* Re:

The body of the memorandum is typed in block form with one line between paragraphs. No salutation or complimentary close is used. The memo may be signed or not, as wished.

Many companies have interoffice envelopes for inhouse communications. External memos are mailed in regularly addressed letterhead envelopes.

WRITING BUSINESS LETTERS

The secretary is often expected to write letters and memorandums for her own signature. The executive may ask her to take care of minor matters on her own initiative. Some employers make a practice of giving a general idea of a response to a correspondent and ask her to write the letter for his signature. Frequently, too, correspondence comes to the office in the absence of the employer that needs to be acknowledged immediately.

For all those situations, it is important for the secretary to develop a clear and correct writing style. Practice is the best teacher of this skill. Following, however, are samples of such communications: acknowledgment, apology, appointment, appreciation, collection, complaint, confirmation, follow-up, introduction, invitation and reply, informal invitation and reply, order, request, reservation, sympathy, and thank you.

Acknowledgment

Dear Mr. Bryan:

Your letter to Mr. Doe in reference to the meeting in Georgia arrived during his absence from the office. I feel sure that he will be pleased at the progress of your arrangements. He is expected back on Monday and will be in touch with you then.

If I can be of any assistance in the meantime, please feel free to call on me.

Sincerely yours,

Apology

Dear Mr. Carter:

Please accept our apology for failing to let you know of the alteration in Mr. Doe's itinerary. The change was quite unexpected, so there was no time for a letter. We tried to reach you by telephone, but you were unavailable.

Mr. Doe plans to be in your area within the next few months and will make a special point of trying to see you then.

Sincerely yours,

Appointment

Dear Mr. Davis:

Mr. Doe will be glad to see you while you are in New York next month. He suggests Wednesday, February 20, at 3 p.m.

Please let me know whether this is convenient for you.

Sincerely yours,

Appreciation

Dear Jean:

I want to thank you in particular and the committee as a whole for your invaluable assistance on Mr. Doe's recent campaign stop in Nebraska. As you know, the program was a huge success, and much of the credit is due to your efforts.

I look forward to working with you again soon.

Sincerely yours,

Collection

Dear Mr. Elton:

Just a friendly reminder that we have not received the March payment on your account.

If your check has already been mailed, please disregard this letter. If not, your early attention to the matter will be appreciated.

Sincerely yours,

Complaint

Gentlemen:

Your statement of April 1 again shows an outstanding charge of $91.50 for an order of calculator tape placed on January 3. This order was canceled on January 10 and thus was never filled.

Enclosed is a copy of our letter of cancellation. Please correct your records accordingly and send us a revised statement.

Very truly yours,

Confirmation

Dear Mr. Frost:

You are right that Mr. Doe will attend the conference in San Francisco on July 20. He expects to arrive in the city about noon and will telephone you then.

Mr. Doe asks me to thank you for including him and to say that he looks forward to meeting with you and your associates.

Sincerely yours,

Follow-up

To: Jane Gray

From: Mary Roe

Re: Expense Report

Mr. Doe asks me to remind you that Mr. Harvard's expense report is due next week. Please be sure that it includes charges for his recent trip to the home office.

Many thanks.

J.G.

Introduction

Dear Jack:

This will introduce my former associate Richard Roe, who is assuming the position of Vice President of Sanford Manufacturing in your city.

I know he would appreciate your introducing him to the business community of Detroit and helping him find his footing in a new city.

Many thanks, Jack, and I hope to see you soon.

Cordially,

Invitation: Formal

Mr. and Mrs. William Lawrence
request the pleasure of the company of
Mr. and Mrs. Philip Montague
at dinner
on Thursday, the tenth of November
at eight o'clock
Fifteen Chestnut Street
Black tie

R.S.V.P.

Reply: Formal

Mr. and Mrs. Philip Montague
accept with pleasure
the kind invitation of
Mr. and Mrs. William Lawrence
to be present at dinner
on Thursday, the tenth of November
at eight o'clock
Fifteen Chestnut Street

Invitation: Informal

Dear Kitty:

Can you get free to have lunch with John Wood and me a week from next Monday, March 5? If so, I'll make reservations at Alfredo's for 1 p.m.

Drop me a note at your convenience. It will be pleasant picking up on our respective doings.

Sincerely yours,

Reply: Informal

Dear Jane:

I'll be delighted to have lunch with you and John on Monday, March 5. I'll see you at 1 p.m. at Alfredo's.

Many thanks. I'll tell you all the gossip then.

Cordially,

Order

To: Supply Specialists

From: Jane Roe, secretary to Mr. Doe

Re: Xstamps

Please enter our order for two check endorsement stamps to be imprinted as follows:
Petroplex Savings Inc.
1234 Denison Street
Dallas, TX 78702
(801) 973-767.

Your catalog shows this item at $54.25 each. Please send the shipment and invoice to my attention. Thank you.

Request

Gentlemen:

Several members of our staff have expressed interest in your company's new lap-style personal computer for traveling businessmen.

Would it be convenient for one of your representatives to demonstrate the instrument in my office one day next week? Tuesday would be best for us. Call me if that is suitable for you and we can set a time.

Very truly yours,

Reservation

Gentlemen:

Please reserve a single room with bath for the nights of August 1 to 5 inclusive in the name of John Doe. Mr. Doe will arrive in Atlanta at 3 p.m. on August 1, on Delta Flight 234 out of New York.

Mr. Doe will also need the use of a meeting room on the afternoon of August 2, and if possible a recording secretary.

I shall appreciate your prompt confirmation of these arrangements.

Very truly yours,

Sympathy

Dear Jean:

All of us in the Advertising Department were saddened at the news of Carol's tragic death. Our association with her over the years was always a bright spot in a workaday world, and we shall miss her sorely.

Sincerely yours,

Thank You

Dear Fred:

I want to thank you for your cordial reception of my friend Jean. Your introduction to your business associates greatly facilitated her trip, and she tells me she made some important contacts.

Thanks again, Fred, and if I can return the favor just call on me.

Cordially,

FORMS OF ADDRESS

Specific forms of address are used for persons holding government, religious, or honorary titles. Although most such positions are now held by both men and women, the following listing gives the correct form for men. For a woman holding the position, merely substitute Madam for Sir, and Mrs., Miss, or Ms. for Mr.

Care should be taken with the terms Honorable and Reverend. These words are adjectives, not titles. For that reason, they may not be followed by the surname alone.

The Honorable John Doe, not The Honorable Doe

The Reverend John Doe, not The Reverend Doe

In conversation, a clergyman is addressed as Dr. or Mr. Doe, never Reverend Doe.

The forms of address listed here include those for the President and Vice President (page 108-109); the Federal Judiciary (pages 109-111); members of Congress (pages 111-114); heads of Congressional agencies (page 114-115); Executive Department officials (pages 115-117); Ambassadors and ministers of the United States and of foreign countries (page 117-119); United Nations officials (pages 119-120); state and local officials (page 120-121); the clergy (pages 121-124); the military (pages 124-125), and Canadian officials (pages 125-127).

THE WHITE HOUSE

The President

Address:

    The President
    The White House
    Washington, DC 20500

Salutation:	Formal:	Mr. President:
	Informal:	Dear Mr. President:
Closing:	Formal:	Most respectfully yours,
	Informal:	Sincerely yours,
In conversation:		Mr. President *or* Sir

The Vice President

Address:		The Vice President
		United States Senate
		Washington, DC 20510
Salutation:	Formal:	Mr. Vice President:
	Informal:	Dear Mr. Vice Presi-dent:
Closing:	Formal:	Very truly yours,
	Informal:	Sincerely yours,
In conversation:		Mr. Vice President *or* Sir

THE FEDERAL JUDICIARY

Chief Justice of the United States

Address:		The Chief Justice of the United States
		The Supreme Court of the United States
		Washington, DC
Salutation:	Formal:	Sir:
	Informal:	Dear Mr. Chief Justice:
Closing:	Formal:	Very truly yours,

Informal: Sincerely yours,
In conversation: Mr. Chief Justice *or* Sir

Associate Justice of the Supreme Court
Address: Mr. Justice (surname
                               only)
                             The Supreme Court of
                               the United States
                             Washington, DC
Salutation: Formal: Sir:
               Informal: Dear Mr. Justice:
Closing: Formal: Very truly yours,
               Informal: Sincerely yours,
In conversation: Mr. Justice *or* Mr. Justice
                               (surname) *or* Sir

Retired Justice of the Supreme Court
Address: The Honorable (full
                               name)
                             (Local address)
Salutation: Formal: Sir:
            Informal: Dear Mr. Justice:
Closing: Formal: Very truly yours,
               Informal: Sincerely yours,

Presiding Justice of Other Federal Courts
Address: The Honorable (full
                               name)

Presiding Justice
(Name of court)
(Local address)

Salutation:	Formal:	Sir:
	Informal:	Dear Mr. Justice:
Closing:	Formal:	Very truly yours,
	Informal:	Sincerely yours,
In conversation:		Mr. Justice or Mr. Justice (surname) or Sir

Judge of a Federal Court

Address:	The Honorable (full name)
	Judge of the (name of court; if a U.S. district court, give district)
	(Local address)
Salutation:	Dear Judge (surname):
Closing:	Sincerely yours,
In conversation:	Judge or Sir

MEMBERS OF CONGRESS

Senator

Address:	The Honorable (full name)
	United States Senate
	Washington, DC

Salutation:	Dear Senator (sur- name):
Closing:	Sincerely yours,
In conversation:	Senator

Committee Chairman, United States Senate

Address:	The Honorable (full name)
	Chairman, Committee on (name)
	United States Senate
	Washington, DC
Salutation:	Dear Mr. Chairman:
Closing:	Sincerely yours,
In conversation:	Mr. Chairman

Subcommittee Chairman, United States Senate

Address:	The Honorable (full name)
	Chairman, Subcommit- tee on (name)
	(Name of full commit- tee)
	United States Senate
	Washington, DC
Salutation:	Dear Senator (sur- name):
Closing:	Sincerely yours,
In conversation:	Mr. Chairman

Speaker of the House of Representatives

Address:		The Honorable (full name)
		United States House of Representatives
		Washington, DC
Salutation:	Formal:	Sir:
	Informal:	Dear Mr. (surname):
Closing:	Formal:	Very truly yours,
	Informal:	Sincerely yours,
In conversation:		Mr. (surname) *or* Sir

Committee Chairman, United States House of Representatives

Address:	The Honorable (full name)
	Chairman, Committee on (name)
	House of Representatives
	Washington, DC
Salutation:	Dear Mr. Chairman:
Closing:	Sincerely yours,
In conversation:	Mr. Chairman

Subcommittee Chairman, United States House of Representatives

Address: The Honorable (full name)
Chairman, Subcommittee on (name)
(Name of full committee)
House of Representatives
Washington, DC

Salutation: Dear Mr. (surname):

Closing: Sincerely yours,

HEADS OF CONGRESSIONAL AGENCIES

Librarian of Congress

Address: The Honorable (full name)
Librarian of Congress
Library of Congress
101 Independence Avenue
Washington, DC 20540

Salutation: Dear Mr. (surname):

Closing: Sincerely yours,

Comptroller General

Address: The Honorable (full name)
Comptroller General of the United States
General Accounting Office
441 G Street NW
Washington, DC 20548

Salutation: Dear Mr. (surname):

Closing: Sincerely yours,

Public Printer

Address: The Honorable (full name)
Public Printer
U.S. Government Printing Office
North Capitol and H Streets NW
Washington, DC 20401

Salutation: Dear Mr. (surname):

Closing: Sincerely yours,

EXECUTIVE DEPARTMENT OFFICIALS

Cabinet Secretaries

Address: The Honorable (full name)

Secretary of (name of
   department)
Washington, DC

Salutation:	Dear Mr. Secretary:
Closing:	Sincerely yours,

Postmaster General

Address:	The Honorable (full name)
	Postmaster General
	Washington, DC
Salutation:	Dear Mr. Postmaster General:
Closing:	Sincerely yours,

Attorney General

Address:	The Honorable (full name)
	The Attorney General
	Constitution Avenue and 10th Street NW
	Washington, DC 20530
Salutation:	Dear Mr. Attorney General:
Closing:	Sincerely yours,

Under Secretary of a Cabinet-rank Department

Address:	The Honorable (full name)

Under Secretary of
(name of department)
Washington, DC

Salutation: Dear Mr. (surname):
Closing: Sincerely yours,

AMBASSADORS AND MINISTERS OF THE UNITED STATES

Ambassador
Address: The Honorable (full name)
Ambassador of the United States (city, country)

Salutation:	Formal:	Dear Mr. Ambassador:
	Informal:	Sir:
Closing:	Formal:	Very truly yours,
	Informal:	Sincerely yours,
In conversation:		Mr. Ambassador *or* Sir

Chargé d'Affaires, Consul General, Consul, or Vice Consul
Address: (Full name), Esq.
(Title)
(City, country)

Salutation:	Formal:	Sir:
	Informal:	Dear Mr. (surname):

Closing:	Formal:	Very truly yours,
	Informal:	Sincerely yours,

FOREIGN AMBASSADORS AND MINISTERS

Ambassador

Address:		His Excellency, (full name)
		Ambassador of (country)
		(Local address)
Salutation:	Formal:	Excellency:
	Informal:	Dear Mr. Ambassador:
Closing:	Formal:	Very truly yours,
	Informal:	Sincerely yours,
In conversation:		Mr. Ambassador *or* Sir

Minister

Address:		The Honorable (full name)
		Minister of (country)
		(Local address)
Salutation:	Formal:	Sir:
	Informal:	Dear Mr . Minister:
Closing:	Formal:	Very truly yours,
	Informal:	Sincerely yours,
In conversation:		Mr. Minister *or* Sir

Foreign Chargé d'Affaires

Address:		Mr. (full name)
		Chargé d'Affaires of (country)

		(Local address)
Salutation:	Formal:	Sir:
	Informal:	Dear Mr. (surname):
Closing:	Formal:	Very truly yours,
	Informal:	Sincerely yours,
In conversation:		Sir *or* Mr. (surname)

UNITED NATIONS OFFICIALS

Secretary General

Address:		His Excellency, (full name)
		Secretary General of the United Nations
		New York, NY 10017
Salutation:	Formal:	Excellency:
	Informal:	Dear Mr. Secretary General:
Closing:	Formal:	Very truly yours,
	Informal:	Sincerely yours,

U.S. Representative with Rank of Ambassador

Address:	The Honorable (full name)
	United States Representative to the United Nations
	New York, NY 10017

Salutation:	Formal:	Sir:
	Informal:	Dear Mr. Ambassador:
Closing:	Formal:	Very truly yours,
	Informal:	Sincerely yours,

Foreign Representative with Rank of Ambassador

Address:		His Excellency, (full name)
		Representative of (country) to the United Nations
		New York, NY 10017
Salutation:	Formal:	Dear Mr. Ambassador:
	Informal:	Excellency:
Closing:	Formal:	Very truly yours,
	Informal:	Sincerely yours,

STATE AND LOCAL OFFICIALS

Governor of a State

Address:		The Honorable (full name)
		Governor of (state)
		(City, state)
Salutation:	Formal:	Sir:
	Informal:	Dear Governor (surname):

| Closing: | Formal: | Respectfully yours, |
| | Informal: | Very sincerely yours, |

Mayor of a City

Address:	The Honorable (full name)
	Mayor of (city)
	City Hall
	(City, state)
Salutation:	Dear Mayor (surname):
Closing:	Sincerely yours,

THE CLERGY

The Pope

Address:	His Holiness (full name)
	Vatican City
Salutation:	Your Holiness:
Closing:	Respectfully yours,
In conversation:	Your Holiness

Cardinal

Address	His Eminence (Christian name) Cardinal (surname)
	Archbishop of (city)
	(City, state)
Salutation:	Formal:	Your Eminence:

121

	Informal:	Dear Cardinal (sur-name):
Closing:	Formal:	Respectfully yours,
	Informal:	Sincerely yours,
In conversation:		Your Eminence

Archbishop
Address:

> The Most Reverend
> (full name)
> Archbishop of (city)
> (City, state)

Salutation:	Formal:	Your Excellency:
	Informal:	Dear Archbishop (surname):
Closing:	Formal:	Respectfully yours,
	Informal:	Sincerely yours,
In conversation:		Your Excellency

Bishop
Address:

> The Most Reverend
> (full name)
> Bishop of (diocese)
> (City, state)

Salutation:	Formal:	Your Excellency:
	Informal:	Dear Bishop (surname):
Closing:	Formal:	Respectfully yours,
	Informal:	Sincerely yours,
In conversation:		Your Excellency

Priest

Address:	The Reverend (full name, followed by initials of his order, if any) (Local address)
Salutation:	Dear Father (surname):
Closing:	Sincerely yours,

Protestant Bishop

Address:		The Right Reverend (full name) Bishop of (bishopric) (Local address)
Salutation:	Formal:	Right Reverend Sir:
	Informal:	Dear Bishop (surname):
Closing:	Formal:	Respectfully yours,
	Informal:	Sincerely yours,

Protestant Minister

Address:		The Reverend (full name) (Address of church) (City, state)
Salutation:	Formal:	Dear Sir:
	Informal:	Dear Dr. or Mister (surname):
Closing:		Sincerely yours,

Rabbi

Address: Rabbi (full name)
                           (Local address)
Salutation: Dear Dr. *or* Rabbi
                           (surname)
Closing: Sincerely yours,

MILITARY OFFICERS
ARMY, AIR FORCE, MARINE CORPS

General, Brigadier General, Major General, Lieutenant General

Address: (Full rank, full name)
                           (Name of service)
                           (Local address)
Salutation: Dear General (sur-
                           name):
Closing: Sincerely yours,

Colonel, Lieutenant Colonel

Address: (Same as above)
Salutation: Dear Colonel:
Closing: Sincerely yours,

Major, Captain, First Lieutenant, Second Lieutenant

Address: (Same as above)
Salutation: Dear (rank) (surname):
Closing: Sincerely yours,

NAVY, COAST GUARD

Admiral, Vice Admiral, Rear Admiral

Address: (Full rank, full name)
                                  (Name of service)
                                  (Local service)

Salutation: Dear Admiral (sur-
                                     name):

Closing: Sincerely yours,

Commodore, Captain, Commander

Address: (Same as above)
Salutation: Dear (rank) (surname):
Closing: Sincerely yours,

All Other Ranks

Address: (Same as above)
Salutation: Dear Mr. (surname):
Closing: Sincerely yours,

CANADA

Prime Minister

Address: The Right Honorable
                                  (full name), P.C., M.P.
                                  Prime Minister of
                                  Canada
                                  Parliament Building
                                  Ottawa, Ontario

Salutation:	Formal:	Sir *or* Dear Sir:
	Informal:	Dear Mr. Prime Minister: *or*
		Dear Mr. (surname):
Closing:	Formal:	Your Excellency's obedient servant,
	Informal:	Yours very sincerely,
In conversation:		Your Excellency

Cabinet Officer

Address:		The Honorable (full name), P.C., M.P. Minister of (department) Ottawa, Ontario
Salutation:	Formal:	Sir: *or* Dear Sir:
	Informal:	Dear Mr. (surname):
In conversation:		Sir *or* Mr. Minister

Member of Parliament

Address:		(Full name), Esq., M.P. House of Commons Ottawa, Ontario
Salutation:	Formal:	Dear Sir:
	Informal:	Dear Mr. (surname):
Closing:		Yours very sincerely,
In conversation:		Sir *or* Mr. (surname)

Mayor

Address:		His Worship
		The Mayor of (city)
		(Local address)
Salutation:	Formal:	Dear Sir:
	Informal:	Dear Mr. Mayor:
Closing:		Yours very sincerely,
In conversation:		Sir *or* Mr. Mayor

CHAPTER V

USEFUL REFERENCES

COMMON ABBREVIATIONS

a .... acre, ampere
AA .... author's alterations
A and M .... agricultural and mechanical
AAR .... against all risks
ab .... about
AB .... (L *artium baccalaureus*) bachelor of
                           arts
abbr .... abbreviation
abr .... abridged
abs .... abstract
ac .... account
acad .... academy
ack .... acknowledgment
acpt .... acceptance
actg .... acting
AD .... anno Domini (often small capitals)
ad int .... ad interim
adj .... adjective, adjustment
adm .... administration
ADP .... automatic data processing
ad val .... ad valorem
advt .... advertisement

afft .... affidavit
AG .... attorney general
agt .... agent
AI .... ad interim
aka .... also known as
alw .... allowance
AM .... ante meridiem (often lowercase)
amb .... ambassador
amdt .... amendment
amp .... ampere
amt .... amount
anc .... ancient
anon .... anonymous
ans .... answer
ant...................... antonym
AP .... additional premium, author's proof
APO .... army post office
app .... appendix
appl .... applied
appt .... appointment
apt .... apartment
AR .... accounts receivable, annual return
arr .... arrival
ASAP .... as soon as possible
asgmt .... assignment
assn .... association
assoc .... associate

asst	assistant
at no	atomic number
att	attached, attention, attorney
attn	attention
atty	attorney
atty gen	attorney general
at wt	atomic weight
aux	auxiliary
AV	ad valorem, audiovisual
avdp	avoirdupois
ave	avenue
avg	average
BA	bachelor of arts
bal	balance
bar	barometric
bbl	barrel, barrels
BC	before Christ (often small capitals)
bd ft	board foot
bet	between
bf	boldface
biog	biography
bk	bank, book
bkg	banking, bookkeeping
bldg	building
blvd	boulevard
BO	back order, box office
bor	borough

BR	bills receivable
bros	brothers
BS	bachelor of science, balance sheet, bill of sale
bu	bureau, bushel
bus	business
ca	circa
CA	chartered accountant, current account
CAD	computer-aided design
CAI	computer-aided instruction
canc	canceled
cap	capacity, capital, capitalize
caps	capitals
cat	catalog
CBI	computer-based instruction
cc	cubic centimeter
CC	carbon copy
cent	centigrade, century
CEO	chief executive officer
cert	certificate, certified
cf	compare
CFO	chief financial officer
chg	change, charge
chm	chairman
CI	certificate of insurance

cld	called, cleared
clk	clerk
cml	commercial
co	company, county
c/o	care of
COD	cash on delivery
coll	collateral
COLA	cost of living adjustment
colloq	colloquial
coml	commercial
compd	compound
conf	conference, confidential
conj	conjunction
consol	consolidated
cp	coupon
CPI	consumer price index
CPM	cost per thousand
cpu	central processing unit
CS	capital stock
ctf	certificate
ctn	carton
cu	cubic
cum	cumulative
cwt	hundredweight
CY	calendar year
dat	dative
db	debenture

DB	daybook
d/b/a	doing business as
deg	degree
dely	delivery
dept	department
diam	diameter
dict	dictionary
dir	director
dis	discount
div	dividend
do	ditto
doc	document
doz	dozen
dup	duplicate
DW	deadweight
ea	each
EEO	equal employment opportunity
e.g.	(L. *exempli gratia*) for example
elev	elevation
emer	emeritus
enc or encl	enclosure
env	envelope
esp	especially
est	established, estimated
ETA	estimated time of arrival
etc	et cetera
ETD	estimated time of departure

et seq	(L. *et sequens*) and the following one
evg	evening
ex	example
exch	exchange
exec	executive
exp	expense, express
fax	facsimile
fcp	foolscap
fed	federation
FIFO	first in, first out
fig	figurative, figure
fin sec	financial secretary
fn	footnote
FOB	free on board
freq	frequency
front	frontispiece
frt	freight
ft	feet, foot
fwd	foreword, forward
FX	foreign exchange
FYI	for your information
gal	gallon
GED	general equivalency diploma
geog	geographic
GIGO	garbage in, garbage out
GMT	Greenwich mean time
govt	government

GPA	grade point average
gram	grammar
gro	gross
gr wt	gross weight
gtd	guaranteed
hdbk	handbook
hdwe	hardware
hgt	height
hon	honorable, honorary
hor	horizontal
hwy	highway
i.e.	(L. *id est*) that is
IG	inspector general
illus	illustrated
in	inch
inc	incorporated
incl	including, inclusive
indef	indefinite
inf	infinitive
inq	inquire
ins	insurance
intl	international
irreg	irregular
ital	italic
Jr	junior
k	karat
lang	language

lat	latitude
lb	(L. *libra*) pound
lc	lowercase
LCD	least common denominator
LCL	less-than-carload lot
ld	load
lf	lightface
LIFO	last in, first out
liq	liquid
lith	lithographic
long	longitude
ltd	limited
lt gov	lieutenant governor
let	letter
lv	leave
MA	(L. *magister artium*) master of arts
mag	magazine, magnitude
man	manual
masc	masculine
max	maximum
mdse	merchandise
mech	mechanical
mfd	manufactured
mfg	manufacturing
MFN	most favored nation
mfr	manufacturer
mgr	manager

mi	mile
min	minute
misc	miscellaneous
mktg	marketing
MLS	master of library science
Mme	(F) madame
MO	mail order, money order
mpg	miles per gallon
mph	miles per hour
MS	manuscript
msg	message
MSW	master of social work
mtge	mortgage
NA	no account, not applicable, not available
natl	national
naut	nautical
NC	no charge, no credit
neg	negative
neut	neuter
NMI	no middle initial
nom	nominative
non seq	non sequitur
num	numeral
obj	object
off	office, officer
OJT	on-the-job training

opp	opposite
org	organization
orig	original
oz	ounce, ounces
p	page
pam	pamphlet
p and g	postage and handling
P and L	profit and loss
par	paragraph
pat	patent
payt	payment
PBX	private branch exchange
PC	percent, percentage, personal computer
pd	paid
PD	per diem
PE	printer's error
P/E	price/earnings
perm	permanent
pert	pertaining
pfd	preferred
pg	page
pkg	package
pkwy	parkway
PM	post meridiem (often lowercase)
pmk	postmark
PN	promissory note

PO .... post office, purchase order
pp .... pages
PP .... parcel post, postpaid, prepaid
ppd .... postpaid, prepaid
pr .... pair, price
PR .... payroll
pref .... preface, preferred
prem .... premium
pres .... present, president
prev .... previously
prf .... proof
prin .... principal
prod .... product, production
prop .... property
PS .... postscript
ptg .... printing
PUD .... pickup and delivery
qty .... quantity
qual .... quality
R .... registered trademark
RAM .... random access memory
R & D .... research and development
rd .... road
rec .... receipt, record
recd .... received
ref .... reference, refund
regd .... registered

rept	report
reqd	required
resp	respective
rev	revenue, revised
ROI	return on investment
ROM	read only memory
RSVP	(F *repondez s'il vous plait*) please reply
rte	route
rtw	ready-to-wear
RV	recreational vehicle
rwy	railway
SAE	self-addressed envelope
SASE	self-addressed stamped envelope
SC	small capitals
SRD	special drawing rights
secy	secretary
ser	serial, series
sgd	signed
shpt	shipment
shtg	shortage
SOP	standard operating procedure
ST	short ton
std	standard
stk	stock
supt	superintendent
svgs	savings

sym	symbol
syn	synonym
syst	system
TBA	to be announced (often lowercase)
tech	technical
temp	temperature
terr	territory
tfr	transfer
tkt	ticket
TM	trademark
TO	table of organization
tpk	turnpike
treas	treasurer, treasury
twp	township
ugt	urgent
unan	unanimous
usu	usual, usually
UW	underwriter
val	value
VAT	value-added tax
VDT	video display terminal
VDU	visual display unit
VHF	very high frequency
VLF	very low frequency
vocab	vocabulary
vou	voucher
vv	vice versa

WATS	Wide-Area Telecommunications Service
WB	waybill
WC	without charge
whse	warehouse
whsle	wholesale
wi	when issued
w/o	without
WPM	words per minute
XC or xcp	ex coupon
XD or x div	ex dividend
XR	ex rights
XW	ex warrants

POSTAL INFORMATION

The U.S. Postal Service offers many and varied mail services. Rates for these services are subject to change. Rates are proposed by the Postal Service and reviewed and approved by the Postal Rate Commission. The principal classes of mail are as follows:

First Class

This service includes letters and other material that is sealed and may not be inspected. First-class mail that weighs more than 11 ounces may be sent as Priority Mail (see below). In addition to letters, first-class mail covers postal cards, postcards, and all other written matter except book manuscripts, magazine articles, music, and manuscript copy with galley proofs.

Express Mail

This service is available for any mailable article up to 70 pounds. Next-day delivery between major U.S. cities is guaranteed or fee is refunded. Time of delivery depends on distance of destination. Second-day delivery is offered for destinations not on the Next Day Delivery Network. In most cities, special street mailboxes are provided for Express Mail. Pick-up service is also available for a nominal additional charge.

Third Class

This service covers packages up to but not including 16 ounces in weight. Materials include publications, small parcels, printed matter, booklets, and catalogs.

Fourth Class-Parcel Post

This service for material weighing 16 ounces and over covers merchandise and printed matter of all types. Packages may be sealed, subject to inspection. Rates are set according to zone.

Priority Mail

This service provides the most expeditious handling and transportation available. Parcels weighing up to 70 pounds and not exceeding 108 inches in length and girth combined are accepted, including written and other material, sealed or unsealed. Rates vary according to zone. See also First Class, above.

SPECIAL DOMESTIC SERVICES

Special Handling

This service is available for third-class and fourth-class parcels at a fee in addition to the postage. Parcels are transported as expeditiously as possible, but not by special delivery.

Special Delivery

This service is available at an additional fee for all classes of mail. The material is delivered immediately upon receipt at the post office.

Registered Mail

This service is available only for first-class items. It provides evidence of mailing. For a further fee it offers evidence of receipt and delivery only to the addressee. Registered mail is useful for mailing such items as deeds, bonds, or stock certificates; money, and jewelry. The value of the item must be declared at time of mailing.

Certification

This service is available for first-class mail having no intrinsic value. A receipt is furnished on mailing, and evidence of delivery is supplied.

Insurance

Coverage is available on third-class and fourth-class mail. Rates vary according to declared value of the parcel, up to a limit of $500. To quality for insurance, first-class and priority mail must be registered.

Private Mail Services

Private transfer services are currently in wide use. Delivery is available overnight, second day, and third day. Material ranging from letters to large packages is accepted. Among the best known are Federal Express, United Parcel Service (UPS), DHL Worldwide Courier Express, and TNT Skypak. Local outlets for these and other services can be found in the Yellow pages telephone directory. Messenger service of various types is widely available. Services include individual pick-up and delivery within the city and between cities and towns in metropolitan areas. These firms also are listed in the Yellow Pages.

STATE ABBREVIATIONS

The following abbreviations for states of the U.S. are approved by the Postal Service. They are intended for use only in addresses on envelopes or other mailing labels. They should not be used as abbreviations in other contexts. In text, for instance, the abbreviation for California should be Calif., not CA.

Alabama .... AL
Alaska .... AK
American Samoa .... AS
Arizona .... AZ
Arkansas .... AR
California .... CA
Canal Zone .... CZ
Colorado .... CO
Connecticut .... CT

Delaware	DE
District of Columbia	DC
Florida	FL
Georgia	GA
Guam	GU
Hawaii	HI
Idaho	ID
Illinois	IL
Indiana	IN
Iowa	IA
Kansas	KS
Kentucky	KY
Louisiana	LA
Maine	ME
Maryland	MD
Massachusetts	MA
Michigan	MI
Minnesota	MN
Missouri	MO
Mississippi	MS
Montana	MT
Nebraska	NE
Nevada	NV
New Hampshire	NH
New Jersey	NJ
New Mexico	NM
New York	NY

PERPETUAL CALENDAR

Choose the year you want in the key. The number opposite the year is the number of the calendar to use for that year:

1776	9	1799	3	1822	3
1777	4	1800	4	1823	4
1778	5	1801	5	1824	12
1779	6	1802	6	1825	7
1780	14	1803	7	1826	1
1781	2	1804	8	1827	2
1782	3	1805	3	1828	10
1783	4	1806	4	1829	5
1784	12	1807	5	1830	6
1785	7	1808	13	1831	7
1786	1	1809	1	1832	8
1787	2	1810	2	1833	3
1788	10	1811	3	1834	4
1789	5	1812	11	1835	5
1790	6	1813	6	1836	13
1791	7	1814	7	1837	1
1792	8	1815	1	1838	2
1793	3	1816	9	1839	3
1794	4	1817	4	1840	11
1795	5	1818	5	1841	6
1796	13	1819	6	1842	7
1797	1	1820	14	1843	1
1798	2	1821	2	1844	9

1845 4	1873 4	1901 3
1846 5	1874 5	1902 4
1847 6	1875 6	1903 5
1848 14	1876 14	1904 13
1849 2	1877 2	1905 1
1850 3	1878 3	1906 2
1851 4	1879 4	1907 3
1852 12	1880 12	1908 11
1853 7	1881 7	1909 6
1854 1	1882 1	1910 7
1855 2	1883 2	1911 1
1856 10	1884 10	1912 9
1857 5	1885 5	1912 9
1858 6	1886 6	1913 4
1859 7	1887 7	1914 5
1860 8	1888 8	1915 6
1861 3	1889 3	1916 14
1862 4	1890 4	1917 2
1863 5	1891 5	1918 3
1864 13	1892 13	1919 4
1865 1	1893 1	1920 12
1866 2	1894 2	1921 7
1867 3	1895 3	1922 1
1868 11	1896 11	1923 2
1869 6	1897 6	1924 10
1870 7	1898 7	1925 5
1871 1	1899 1	1926 6
1872 9	1900 2	1927 7

1928 8	1956 8	1984 8
1929 3	1957 3	1985 3
1930 4	1958 4	1986 4
1931 5	1959 5	1987 5
1932 13	1960 13	1988 13
1933 1	1961 1	1989 1
1934 2	1962 2	1990 2
1935 3	1963 3	1991 3
1936 11	1964 11	1992 11
1937 6	1965 6	1993 6
1938 7	1966 7	1994 7
1939 1	1967 1	1995 1
1940 9	1968 9	1996 9
1941 4	1969 4	1997 4
1942 5	1970 5	1998 5
1943 6	1971 6	1999 6
1944 14	1972 14	2000 14
1945 2	1973 2	2001 2
1946 3	1974 3	2003 4
1947 4	1975 4	2005 7
1948 12	1976 12	2006 1
1949 7	1977 7	2007 2
1950 1	1978 1	2008 10
1951 2	1979 2	2009 5
1952 10	1980 10	2010 6
1953 5	1981 5	2011 7
1954 6	1982 6	2012 8
1955 7	1983 7	2013 3

1

JANUARY						
S	M	T	W	T	F	S
1	2	3	4	5	6	7
8	9	10	11	12	13	14
15	16	17	18	19	20	21
22	23	24	25	26	27	28
29	30	31				

MAY						
S	M	T	W	T	F	S
	1	2	3	4	5	6
7	8	9	10	11	12	13
14	15	16	17	18	19	20
21	22	23	24	25	26	27
28	29	30	31			

SEPTEMBER						
S	M	T	W	T	F	S
					1	2
3	4	5	6	7	8	9
10	11	12	13	14	15	16
17	18	19	20	21	22	23
24	25	26	27	28	29	30

FEBRUARY						
S	M	T	W	T	F	S
			1	2	3	4
5	6	7	8	9	10	11
12	13	14	15	16	17	18
19	20	21	22	23	24	25
26	27	28				

JUNE						
S	M	T	W	T	F	S
				1	2	3
4	5	6	7	8	9	10
11	12	13	14	15	16	17
18	19	20	21	22	23	24
25	26	27	28	29	30	

OCTOBER						
S	M	T	W	T	F	S
1	2	3	4	5	6	7
8	9	10	11	12	13	14
15	16	17	18	19	20	21
22	23	24	25	26	27	28
29	30	31				

MARCH						
S	M	T	W	T	F	S
			1	2	3	4
5	6	7	8	9	10	11
12	13	14	15	16	17	18
19	20	21	22	23	24	25
26	27	28	29	30	31	

JULY						
S	M	T	W	T	F	S
						1
2	3	4	5	6	7	8
9	10	11	12	13	14	15
16	17	18	19	20	21	22
23	24	25	26	27	28	29
30	31					

NOVEMBER						
S	M	T	W	T	F	S
			1	2	3	4
5	6	7	8	9	10	11
12	13	14	15	16	17	18
19	20	21	22	23	24	25
26	27	28	29	30		

APRIL						
S	M	T	W	T	F	S
						1
2	3	4	5	6	7	8
9	10	11	12	13	14	15
16	17	18	19	20	21	22
23	24	25	26	27	28	29
30						

AUGUST						
S	M	T	W	T	F	S
		1	2	3	4	5
6	7	8	9	10	11	12
13	14	15	16	17	18	19
20	21	22	23	24	25	26
27	28	29	30	31		

DECEMBER						
S	M	T	W	T	F	S
					1	2
3	4	5	6	7	8	9
10	11	12	13	14	15	16
17	18	19	20	21	22	23
24	25	26	27	28	29	30
31						

2

JANUARY

S	M	T	W	T	F	S
	1	2	3	4	5	6
7	8	9	10	11	12	13
14	15	16	17	18	19	20
21	22	23	24	25	26	27
28	29	30	31			

MAY

S	M	T	W	T	F	S
		1	2	3	4	5
6	7	8	9	10	11	12
13	14	15	16	17	18	19
20	21	22	23	24	25	26
27	28	29	30	31		

SEPTEMBER

S	M	T	W	T	F	S
						1
2	3	4	5	6	7	8
9	10	11	12	13	14	15
16	17	18	19	20	21	22
23	24	25	26	27	28	29
30						

FEBRUARY

S	M	T	W	T	F	S
					1	2	3
4	5	6	7	8	9	10
11	12	13	14	15	16	17
18	19	20	21	22	23	24
25	26	27	28			

JUNE

S	M	T	W	T	F	S
					1	2
3	4	5	6	7	8	9
10	11	12	13	14	15	16
17	18	19	20	21	22	23
24	25	26	27	28	29	30

OCTOBER

S	M	T	W	T	F	S
	1	2	3	4	5	6
7	8	9	10	11	12	13
14	15	16	17	18	19	20
21	22	23	24	25	26	27
28	29	30	31			

MARCH

S	M	T	W	T	F	S
				1	2	3
4	5	6	7	8	9	10
11	12	13	14	15	16	17
18	19	20	21	22	23	24
25	26	27	28	29	30	31

JULY

S	M	T	W	T	F	S
1	2	3	4	5	6	7
8	9	10	11	12	13	14
15	16	17	18	19	20	21
22	23	24	25	26	27	28
29	30	31				

NOVEMBER

S	M	T	W	T	F	S
				1	2	3
4	5	6	7	8	9	10
11	12	13	14	15	16	17
18	19	20	21	22	23	24
25	26	27	28	29	30	

APRIL

S	M	T	W	T	F	S
1	2	3	4	5	6	7
8	9	10	11	12	13	14
15	16	17	18	19	20	21
22	23	24	25	26	27	28
29	30					

AUGUST

S	M	T	W	T	F	S
			1	2	3	4
5	6	7	8	9	10	11
12	13	14	15	16	17	18
19	20	21	22	23	24	25
26	27	28	29	30	31	

DECEMBER

S	M	T	W	T	F	S
						1
2	3	4	5	6	7	8
9	10	11	12	13	14	15
16	17	18	19	20	21	22
23	24	25	26	27	28	29
30	31					

3

JANUARY

S	M	T	W	T	F	S
		1	2	3	4	5
6	7	8	9	10	11	12
13	14	15	16	17	18	19
20	21	22	23	24	25	26
27	28	29	30	31		

MAY

S	M	T	W	T	F	S
			1	2	3	4
5	6	7	8	9	10	11
12	13	14	15	16	17	18
19	20	21	22	23	24	25
26	27	28	29	30	31	

SEPTEMBER

S	M	T	W	T	F	S
1	2	3	4	5	6	7
8	9	10	11	12	13	14
15	16	17	18	19	20	21
22	23	24	25	26	27	28
29	30					

FEBRUARY

S	M	T	W	T	F	S
					1	2
3	4	5	6	7	8	9
10	11	12	13	14	15	16
17	18	19	20	21	22	23
24	25	26	27	28		

JUNE

S	M	T	W	T	F	S
						1
2	3	4	5	6	7	8
9	10	11	12	12	14	15
16	17	18	19	20	21	22
23	24	25	26	27	28	29
30						

OCTOBER

S	M	T	W	T	F	S
		1	2	3	4	5
6	7	8	9	10	11	12
13	14	15	16	17	18	19
20	21	22	23	24	25	26
27	28	29	30	31		

MARCH

S	M	T	W	T	F	S
					1	2
3	4	5	6	7	8	9
10	11	12	13	14	15	16
17	18	19	20	21	22	23
24	25	26	27	28	29	30
31						

JULY

S	M	T	W	T	F	S
	1	2	3	4	5	6
7	8	9	10	11	12	13
14	15	16	17	18	19	20
21	22	23	24	25	26	27
28	29	30	31			

NOVEMBER

S	M	T	W	T	F	S
					1	2
3	4	5	6	7	8	9
10	11	12	13	14	15	16
17	18	19	20	21	22	23
24	25	26	27	28	29	30

APRIL

S	M	T	W	T	F	S
	1	2	3	4	5	6
7	8	9	10	11	12	13
14	15	16	17	18	19	20
21	22	23	24	25	26	27
28	29	30				

AUGUST

S	M	T	W	T	F	S
				1	2	3
4	5	6	7	8	9	10
11	12	13	14	15	16	17
18	19	20	21	22	23	24
25	26	27	28	29	30	31

DECEMBER

S	M	T	W	T	F	S
1	2	3	4	5	6	7
8	9	10	11	12	13	14
15	16	17	18	19	20	21
22	23	24	25	26	27	28
29	30	31				

4

JANUARY

S	M	T	W	T	F	S
			1	2	3	4
5	6	7	8	9	10	11
12	13	14	15	16	17	18
19	20	21	22	23	24	25
26	27	28	29	30	31	

MAY

S	M	T	W	T	F	S
				1	2	3
4	5	6	7	8	9	10
11	12	13	14	15	16	17
18	19	20	21	22	23	24
25	26	27	28	29	30	31

SEPTEMBER

S	M	T	W	T	F	S
	1	2	3	4	5	6
7	8	9	10	11	12	13
14	15	16	17	18	19	20
21	22	23	24	25	26	27
28	29	30				

FEBRUARY

S	M	T	W	T	F	S
						1
2	3	4	5	6	7	8
9	10	11	12	13	14	15
16	17	18	19	20	21	22
23	24	25	26	27	28	

JUNE

S	M	T	W	T	F	S
1	2	3	4	5	6	7
8	9	10	11	12	13	14
15	16	17	18	19	20	21
22	23	24	25	26	27	28
29	30					

OCTOBER

S	M	T	W	T	F	S
			1	2	3	4
5	6	7	8	9	10	11
12	13	14	15	16	17	18
19	20	21	22	23	24	25
26	27	28	29	30	31	

MARCH

S	M	T	W	T	F	S
						1
2	3	4	5	6	7	8
9	10	11	12	13	14	15
16	17	18	19	20	21	22
23	24	25	26	27	28	29
30	31					

JULY

S	M	T	W	T	F	S
		1	2	3	4	5
6	7	8	9	10	11	12
13	14	15	16	17	18	19
20	21	22	23	24	25	26
27	28	29	30	31		

NOVEMBER

S	M	T	W	T	F	S
						1
2	3	4	5	6	7	8
9	10	11	12	13	14	15
16	17	18	19	20	21	22
23	24	25	26	27	28	29
30						

APRIL

S	M	T	W	T	F	S
		1	2	3	4	5
6	7	8	9	10	11	12
13	14	15	16	17	18	19
20	21	22	23	24	25	26
27	28	29	30			

AUGUST

S	M	T	W	T	F	S
					1	2
3	4	5	6	7	8	9
10	11	12	13	14	15	16
17	18	19	20	21	22	23
24	25	26	27	28	29	30
31						

DECEMBER

S	M	T	W	T	F	S
	1	2	3	4	5	6
7	8	9	10	11	12	13
14	15	16	17	18	19	20
21	22	23	24	25	26	27
28	29	30	31			

5

JANUARY

S	M	T	W	T	F	S
				1	2	3
4	5	6	7	8	9	10
11	12	13	14	15	16	17
18	19	20	21	22	23	24
25	26	27	28	29	30	31

MAY

S	M	T	W	T	F	S
					1	2
3	4	5	6	7	8	9
10	11	12	13	14	15	16
17	18	19	20	21	22	23
24	25	26	27	28	29	30
31						

SEPTEMBER

S	M	T	W	T	F	S
		1	2	3	4	5
6	7	8	9	10	11	12
13	14	15	16	17	18	19
20	21	22	23	24	25	26
27	28	29	30			

FEBRUARY

S	M	T	W	T	F	S
1	2	3	4	5	6	7
8	9	10	11	12	13	14
15	16	17	18	19	20	21
16	17	18	19	20	21	22
22	23	24	25	26	27	28

JUNE

S	M	T	W	T	F	S
	1	2	3	4	5	6
7	8	9	10	11	12	13
14	15	16	17	18	19	20
21	22	23	24	25	26	27
28	29	30				

OCTOBER

S	M	T	W	T	F	S
				1	2	3
4	5	6	7	8	9	10
11	12	13	14	15	16	17
18	19	20	21	22	23	24
25	26	27	28	29	30	31

MARCH

S	M	T	W	T	F	S
1	2	3	4	5	6	7
8	9	10	11	12	13	14
15	16	17	18	19	20	21
22	23	24	25	26	27	28
29	30	31				

JULY

S	M	T	W	T	F	S
			1	2	3	4
5	6	7	8	9	10	11
12	13	14	15	16	17	18
19	20	21	22	23	24	25
26	27	28	29	30	31	

NOVEMBER

S	M	T	W	T	F	S
1	2	3	4	5	6	7
8	9	10	11	12	13	14
15	16	17	18	19	20	21
22	23	24	25	26	27	28
29	30					

APRIL

S	M	T	W	T	F	S
			1	2	3	4
5	6	7	8	9	10	11
12	13	14	15	16	17	18
19	20	21	22	23	24	25
26	27	28	29	30		

AUGUST

S	M	T	W	T	F	S
						1
2	3	4	5	6	7	8
9	10	11	12	13	14	15
16	17	18	19	20	21	22
23	24	25	26	27	28	29
30	31					

DECEMBER

S	M	T	W	T	F	S
		1	2	3	4	5
6	7	8	9	10	11	12
13	14	15	16	17	18	19
20	21	22	23	24	25	26
27	28	29	30	31		

6

JANUARY						
S	M	T	W	T	F	S
					1	2
3	4	5	6	7	8	9
10	11	12	13	14	15	16
17	18	19	20	21	22	23
24	25	26	27	28	29	30
31						

MAY						
S	M	T	W	T	F	S
						1
2	3	4	5	6	7	8
9	10	11	12	13	14	15
16	17	18	19	20	21	22
23	24	25	26	27	28	29
30	31					

SEPTEMBER						
S	M	T	W	T	F	S
			1	2	3	4
5	6	7	8	9	10	11
12	13	14	15	16	17	18
19	20	21	22	23	24	25
26	27	28	29	30		

FEBRUARY						
S	M	T	W	T	F	S
	1	2	3	4	5	6
7	8	9	10	11	12	13
14	15	16	17	18	19	20
21	22	23	24	25	26	27
28	29	30				

JUNE						
S	M	T	W	T	F	S
		1	2	3	4	5
6	7	8	9	10	11	12
13	14	15	16	17	18	19
20	21	22	23	24	25	26
27	28	29	30			

OCTOBER						
S	M	T	W	T	F	S
					1	2
3	4	5	6	7	8	9
10	11	12	13	14	15	16
17	18	19	20	21	22	23
24	25	26	27	28	29	30
31						

MARCH						
S	M	T	W	T	F	S
	1	2	3	4	5	6
7	8	9	10	11	12	13
14	15	16	17	18	19	20
21	22	23	24	25	26	27
28	29	30	31			

JULY						
S	M	T	W	T	F	S
				1	2	3
4	5	6	7	8	9	10
11	12	13	14	15	16	17
18	19	20	21	22	23	24
25	26	27	28	29	30	31

NOVEMBER						
S	M	T	W	T	F	S
	1	2	3	4	5	6
7	8	9	10	11	12	13
14	15	16	17	18	19	20
21	22	23	24	25	26	27
28	29	30				

APRIL						
S	M	T	W	T	F	S
				1	2	3
4	5	6	7	8	9	10
11	12	13	14	15	16	17
18	19	20	21	22	23	24
25	26	27	28	29	30	

AUGUST						
S	M	T	W	T	F	S
1	2	3	4	5	6	7
8	9	10	11	12	13	14
15	16	17	18	19	20	21
22	23	24	25	26	27	28
29	30	31				

DECEMBER						
S	M	T	W	T	F	S
			1	2	3	4
5	6	7	8	9	10	11
12	13	14	15	16	17	18
19	20	21	22	23	24	25
26	27	28	29	30	31	

7

JANUARY

S	M	T	W	T	F	S
						1
2	3	4	5	6	7	8
9	10	11	12	13	14	15
16	17	18	19	20	21	22
23	24	25	26	27	28	29
30	31					

MAY

S	M	T	W	T	F	S
1	2	3	4	5	6	7
8	9	10	11	12	13	14
15	16	17	18	19	20	21
22	23	24	25	26	27	28
29	30	31				

SEPTEMBER

S	M	T	W	T	F	S
					1	2	3
4	5	6	7	8	9	10
11	12	13	14	15	16	17
18	19	20	21	22	23	24
25	26	27	28	29	30	

FEBRUARY

S	M	T	W	T	F	S
		1	2	3	4	5
6	7	8	9	10	11	12
13	14	15	16	17	18	19
20	21	22	23	24	25	26
27	28					

JUNE

S	M	T	W	T	F	S
			1	2	3	4
5	6	7	8	9	10	11
12	13	14	15	16	17	18
19	20	21	22	23	24	25
26	27	28	29	30		

OCTOBER

S	M	T	W	T	F	S
						1
2	3	4	5	6	7	8
9	10	11	12	13	14	15
16	17	18	19	20	21	22
23	24	25	26	27	28	29
30	31					

MARCH

S	M	T	W	T	F	S
		1	2	3	4	5
6	7	8	9	10	11	12
13	14	15	16	17	18	19
20	21	22	23	24	25	26
27	28	29	30	31		

JULY

S	M	T	W	T	F	S
					1	2
3	4	5	6	7	8	9
10	11	12	13	14	15	16
17	18	19	20	21	22	23
24	25	26	27	28	29	30
31						

NOVEMBER

S	M	T	W	T	F	S
		1	2	3	4	5
6	7	8	9	10	11	12
13	14	15	16	17	18	19
20	21	22	23	24	25	26
27	28	29	30			

APRIL

S	M	T	W	T	F	S
					1	2
3	4	5	6	7	8	9
10	11	12	13	14	15	16
17	18	19	20	21	22	23
24	25	26	27	28	29	30

AUGUST

S	M	T	W	T	F	S
	1	2	3	4	5	6
7	8	9	10	11	12	13
14	15	16	17	18	19	20
21	22	23	24	25	26	27
28	29	30	31			

DECEMBER

S	M	T	W	T	F	S
				1	2	3
4	5	6	7	8	9	10
11	12	13	14	15	16	17
18	19	20	21	22	23	24
25	26	27	28	29	30	31

8

JANUARY
S	M	T	W	T	F	S
1	2	3	4	5	6	7
8	9	10	11	12	13	14
15	16	17	18	19	20	21
22	23	24	25	26	27	28
29	30	31				

MAY
S	M	T	W	T	F	S
		1	2	3	4	5
6	7	8	9	10	11	12
13	14	15	16	17	18	19
20	21	22	23	24	25	26
27	28	29	30	31		

SEPTEMBER
S	M	T	W	T	F	S
						1
2	3	4	5	6	7	8
9	10	11	12	13	14	15
16	17	18	19	20	21	22
23	24	25	26	27	28	29
30						

FEBRUARY
S	M	T	W	T	F	S
			1	2	3	4
5	6	7	8	9	10	11
12	13	14	15	16	17	18
19	20	21	22	23	24	25
26	27	28	29			

JUNE
S	M	T	W	T	F	S
					1	2
3	4	5	6	7	8	9
10	11	12	13	14	15	16
17	18	19	20	21	22	23
24	25	26	27	28	29	30

OCTOBER
S	M	T	W	T	F	S
	1	2	3	4	5	6
7	8	9	10	11	12	13
14	15	16	17	18	19	20
21	22	23	24	25	26	27
28	29	30	31			

MARCH
S	M	T	W	T	F	S
				1	2	3
4	5	6	7	8	9	10
11	12	13	14	15	16	17
18	19	20	21	22	23	24
25	26	27	28	29	30	31

JULY
S	M	T	W	T	F	S
1	2	3	4	5	6	7
8	9	10	11	12	13	14
15	16	17	18	19	20	21
22	23	24	25	26	27	28
29	30	31				

NOVEMBER
S	M	T	W	T	F	S
				1	2	3
4	5	6	7	8	9	10
11	12	13	14	15	16	17
18	19	20	21	22	23	24
25	26	27	28	29	30	

APRIL
S	M	T	W	T	F	S
1	2	3	4	5	6	7
8	9	10	11	12	13	14
15	16	17	18	19	20	21
22	23	24	25	26	27	28
29	30					

AUGUST
S	M	T	W	T	F	S
			1	2	3	4
5	6	7	8	9	10	11
12	13	14	15	16	17	18
19	20	21	22	23	24	25
26	27	28	29	30	31	

DECEMBER
S	M	T	W	T	F	S
						1
2	3	4	5	6	7	8
9	10	11	12	13	14	15
16	17	18	19	20	21	22
23	24	25	26	27	28	29
30	31					

9

JANUARY

S	M	T	W	T	F	S
	1	2	3	4	5	6
7	8	9	10	11	12	13
14	15	16	17	18	19	20
21	22	23	24	25	26	27
28	29	30	31			

MAY

S	M	T	W	T	F	S
			1	2	3	4
5	6	7	8	9	10	11
12	13	14	15	16	17	18
19	20	21	22	23	24	25
26	27	28	29	30	31	

SEPTEMBER

S	M	T	W	T	F	S
1	2	3	4	5	6	7
8	9	10	11	12	13	14
15	16	17	18	19	20	21
22	23	24	25	26	27	28
29	30					

FEBRUARY

S	M	T	W	T	F	S
				1	2	3
4	5	6	7	8	9	10
11	12	13	14	15	16	17
18	19	20	21	22	23	24
25	26	27	28	29		

JUNE

S	M	T	W	T	F	S
						1
2	3	4	5	6	7	8
9	10	11	12	13	14	15
16	17	18	19	20	21	22
23	24	25	26	27	28	29
30						

OCTOBER

S	M	T	W	T	F	S
		1	2	3	4	5
6	7	8	9	10	11	12
13	14	15	16	17	18	19
20	21	22	23	24	25	26
27	28	29	30	31		

MARCH

S	M	T	W	T	F	S
					1	2
3	4	5	6	7	8	9
10	11	12	13	14	15	16
17	18	19	20	21	22	23
24	25	26	27	28	29	30
31						

JULY

S	M	T	W	T	F	S
	1	2	3	4	5	6
7	8	9	10	11	12	13
14	15	16	17	18	19	20
21	22	23	24	25	26	27
28	29	30	31			

NOVEMBER

S	M	T	W	T	F	S
					1	2
3	4	5	6	7	8	9
10	11	12	13	14	15	16
17	18	19	20	21	22	23
24	25	26	27	28	29	30

APRIL

S	M	T	W	T	F	S
	1	2	3	4	5	6
7	8	9	10	11	12	13
14	15	16	17	18	19	20
21	22	23	24	25	26	27
28	29	30				

AUGUST

S	M	T	W	T	F	S
				1	2	3
4	5	6	7	8	9	10
11	12	13	14	15	16	17
18	19	20	21	22	23	24
25	26	27	28	29	30	31

DECEMBER

S	M	T	W	T	F	S
1	2	3	4	5	6	7
8	9	10	11	12	13	14
15	16	17	18	19	20	21
22	23	24	25	26	27	28
29	30	31				

10

JANUARY

S	M	T	W	T	F	S
		1	2	3	4	5
6	7	8	9	10	11	12
13	14	15	16	17	18	19
20	21	22	23	24	25	26
27	28	29	30	31		

FEBRUARY

S	M	T	W	T	F	S
					1	2
3	4	5	6	7	8	9
10	11	12	13	14	15	16
17	18	19	20	21	22	23
24	25	26	27	28	29	

MARCH

S	M	T	W	T	F	S
						1
2	3	4	5	6	7	8
9	10	11	12	13	14	15
16	17	18	19	20	21	22
23	24	25	26	27	28	29
30	31					

APRIL

S	M	T	W	T	F	S
		1	2	3	4	5
6	7	8	9	10	11	12
13	14	15	16	17	18	19
20	21	22	23	24	25	26
27	28	29	30			

MAY

S	M	T	W	T	F	S
				1	2	3
4	5	6	7	8	9	10
11	12	13	14	15	16	17
18	19	20	21	22	23	24
25	26	27	28	29	30	31

JUNE

S	M	T	W	T	F	S
1	2	3	4	5	6	7
8	9	10	11	12	13	14
15	16	17	18	19	20	21
22	23	24	25	26	27	28
29	30					

JULY

S	M	T	W	T	F	S
		1	2	3	4	5
6	7	8	9	10	11	12
13	14	15	16	17	18	19
20	21	22	23	24	25	26
27	28	29	30	31		

AUGUST

S	M	T	W	T	F	S
					1	2
3	4	5	6	7	8	9
10	11	12	13	14	15	16
17	18	19	20	21	22	23
24	25	26	27	28	29	30
31						

SEPTEMBER

S	M	T	W	T	F	S
	1	2	3	4	5	6
7	8	9	10	11	12	13
14	15	16	17	18	19	20
21	22	23	24	25	26	27
28	29	30				

OCTOBER

S	M	T	W	T	F	S
			1	2	3	4
5	6	7	8	9	10	11
12	13	14	15	16	17	18
19	20	21	22	23	24	25
26	27	28	29	30	31	

NOVEMBER

S	M	T	W	T	F	S
						1
2	3	4	5	6	7	8
9	10	11	12	13	14	15
16	17	18	19	20	21	22
23	24	25	26	27	28	29
30						

DECEMBER

S	M	T	W	T	F	S
	1	2	3	4	5	6
7	8	9	10	11	12	13
14	15	16	17	18	19	20
21	22	23	24	25	26	27
28	29	30	31			

11

JANUARY

S	M	T	W	T	F	S
			1	2	3	4
5	6	7	8	9	10	11
12	13	14	15	16	17	18
19	20	21	22	23	24	25
26	27	28	29	30	31	

MAY

S	M	T	W	T	F	S
					1	2
3	4	5	6	7	8	9
10	11	12	13	14	15	16
17	18	19	20	21	22	23
24	25	26	27	28	29	30
31						

SEPTEMBER

S	M	T	W	T	F	S
		1	2	3	4	5
6	7	8	9	10	11	12
13	14	15	16	17	18	19
20	21	22	23	24	25	26
27	28	29	30			

FEBRUARY

S	M	T	W	T	F	S
						1
2	3	4	5	6	7	8
9	10	11	12	13	14	15
16	17	18	19	20	21	22
23	24	25	26	27	28	29

JUNE

S	M	T	W	T	F	S
	1	2	3	4	5	6
7	8	9	10	11	12	13
14	15	16	17	18	19	20
21	22	23	24	25	26	27
28	29	30				

OCTOBER

S	M	T	W	T	F	S
				1	2	3
4	5	6	7	8	9	10
11	12	13	14	15	16	17
18	19	20	21	22	23	24
25	26	27	28	29	30	31

MARCH

S	M	T	W	T	F	S
1	2	3	4	5	6	7
8	9	10	11	12	13	14
15	16	17	18	19	20	21
22	23	24	25	26	27	28
29	30	31				

JULY

S	M	T	W	T	F	S
			1	2	3	4
5	6	7	8	9	10	11
12	13	14	15	16	17	18
19	20	21	22	23	24	25
26	27	28	29	30	31	

NOVEMBER

S	M	T	W	T	F	S
1	2	3	4	5	6	7
8	9	10	11	12	13	14
15	16	17	18	19	20	21
22	23	24	25	26	27	28
29	30					

APRIL

S	M	T	W	T	F	S
			1	2	3	4
5	6	7	8	9	10	11
12	13	14	15	16	17	18
19	20	21	22	23	24	25
26	27	28	29	30		

AUGUST

S	M	T	W	T	F	S
						1
2	3	4	5	6	7	8
9	10	11	12	13	14	15
16	17	18	19	20	21	22
23	24	25	26	27	28	29
30	31					

DECEMBER

S	M	T	W	T	F	S
		1	2	3	4	5
6	7	8	9	10	11	12
13	14	15	16	17	18	19
20	21	22	23	24	25	26
27	28	29	30	31		

12

JANUARY

S	M	T	W	T	F	S
				1	2	3
4	5	6	7	8	9	10
11	12	13	14	15	16	17
18	19	20	21	22	23	24
25	26	27	28	29	30	31

MAY

S	M	T	W	T	F	S
						1
2	3	4	5	6	7	8
9	10	11	12	13	14	15
16	17	18	19	20	21	22
23	24	25	26	27	28	29
30	31					

SEPTEMBER

S	M	T	W	T	F	S
			1	2	3	4
5	6	7	8	9	10	11
12	13	14	15	16	17	18
19	20	21	22	23	24	25
26	27	28	29	30		

FEBRUARY

S	M	T	W	T	F	S
1	2	3	4	5	6	7
8	9	10	11	12	13	14
15	16	17	18	19	20	21
22	23	24	25	26	27	28
29						

JUNE

S	M	T	W	T	F	S
		1	2	3	4	5
6	7	8	9	10	11	12
13	14	15	16	17	18	19
20	21	22	23	24	25	26
27	28	29	30			

OCTOBER

S	M	T	W	T	F	S
					1	2
3	4	5	6	7	8	9
10	11	12	13	14	15	16
17	18	19	20	21	22	23
24	25	26	27	28	29	30
31						

MARCH

S	M	T	W	T	F	S
	1	2	3	4	5	6
7	8	9	10	11	12	13
14	15	16	17	18	19	20
21	22	23	24	25	26	27
28	29	30	31			

JULY

S	M	T	W	T	F	S
				1	2	3
4	5	6	7	8	9	10
11	12	13	14	15	16	17
18	19	20	21	22	23	24
25	26	27	28	29	30	31

NOVEMBER

S	M	T	W	T	F	S
	1	2	3	4	5	6
7	8	9	10	11	12	13
14	15	16	17	18	19	20
21	22	23	24	25	26	27
28	29	30				

APRIL

S	M	T	W	T	F	S
				1	2	3
4	5	6	7	8	9	10
11	12	13	14	15	16	17
18	19	20	21	22	23	24
25	26	27	28	29	30	

AUGUST

S	M	T	W	T	F	S
1	2	3	4	5	6	7
8	9	10	11	12	13	14
15	16	17	18	19	20	21
22	23	24	25	26	27	28
29	30	31				

DECEMBER

S	M	T	W	T	F	S
			1	2	3	4
5	6	7	8	9	10	11
12	13	14	15	16	17	18
19	20	21	22	23	24	25
26	27	28	29	30	31	

13

JANUARY

S	M	T	W	T	F	S
					1	2
3	4	5	6	7	8	9
10	11	12	13	14	15	16
17	18	19	20	21	22	23
24	25	26	27	28	29	30
31						

MAY

S	M	T	W	T	F	S
1	2	3	4	5	6	7
8	9	10	11	12	13	14
15	16	17	18	19	20	21
22	23	24	25	26	27	28
29	30	31				

SEPTEMBER

S	M	T	W	T	F	S
				1	2	3
4	5	6	7	8	9	10
11	12	13	14	15	16	17
18	19	20	21	22	23	24
25	26	27	28	29	30	

FEBRUARY

S	M	T	W	T	F	S
	1	2	3	4	5	6
7	8	9	10	11	12	13
14	15	16	17	18	19	20
21	22	23	24	25	26	27
28	29					

JUNE

S	M	T	W	T	F	S
			1	2	3	4
5	6	7	8	9	10	11
12	13	14	15	16	17	18
19	20	21	22	23	24	25
26	27	28	29	30		

OCTOBER

S	M	T	W	T	F	S
						1
2	3	4	5	6	7	8
9	10	11	12	13	14	15
16	17	18	19	20	21	22
23	24	25	26	27	28	29
30	31					

MARCH

S	M	T	W	T	F	S
		1	2	3	4	5
6	7	8	9	10	11	12
13	14	15	16	17	18	19
20	21	22	23	24	25	26
27	28	29	30	31		

JULY

S	M	T	W	T	F	S
					1	2
3	4	5	6	7	8	9
10	11	12	13	14	15	16
17	18	19	20	21	22	23
24	25	26	27	28	29	30
31						

NOVEMBER

S	M	T	W	T	F	S
		1	2	3	4	5
6	7	8	9	10	11	12
13	14	15	16	17	18	19
20	21	22	23	24	25	26
27	28	29	30			

APRIL

S	M	T	W	T	F	S
					1	2
3	4	5	6	7	8	9
10	11	12	13	14	15	16
17	18	19	20	21	22	23
24	25	26	27	28	29	30

AUGUST

S	M	T	W	T	F	S
	1	2	3	4	5	6
7	8	9	10	11	12	13
14	15	16	17	18	19	20
21	22	23	24	25	26	27
28	29	30	31			

DECEMBER

S	M	T	W	T	F	S
				1	2	3
4	5	6	7	8	9	10
11	12	13	14	15	16	17
18	19	20	21	22	23	24
25	26	27	28	29	30	31

14

JANUARY

S	M	T	W	T	F	S
						1
2	3	4	5	6	7	8
9	10	11	12	13	14	15
16	17	18	19	20	21	22
23	24	25	26	27	28	29
30	31					

MAY

S	M	T	W	T	F	S
1	2	3	4	5	6
7	8	9	10	11	12	13
14	15	16	17	18	19	20
21	22	23	24	25	26	27
28	29	30	31			
30	31					

SEPTEMBER

S	M	T	W	T	F	S
					1	2
3	4	5	6	7	8	9
10	11	12	13	14	15	16
17	18	19	20	21	22	23
24	25	26	27	28	29	30

FEBRUARY

S	M	T	W	T	F	S
		1	2	3	4	5
6	7	8	9	10	11	12
13	14	15	16	17	18	19
20	21	22	23	24	25	26
27	28	29				

JUNE

S	M	T	W	T	F	S
				1	2	3
4	5	6	7	8	9	10
11	12	13	14	15	16	17
18	19	20	21	22	23	24
25	26	27	28	29	30	

OCTOBER

S	M	T	W	T	F	S
1	2	3	4	5	6	7
8	9	10	11	12	13	14
15	16	17	18	19	20	21
22	23	24	25	26	27	28
29	30	31				

MARCH

S	M	T	W	T	F	S
			1	2	3	4
5	6	7	8	9	10	11
12	13	14	15	16	17	18
19	20	21	22	23	24	25
26	27	28	29	30	31	

JULY

S	M	T	W	T	F	S
						1
2	3	4	5	6	7	8
9	10	11	12	13	14	15
16	17	18	19	20	21	22
23	24	25	26	27	28	29
30	31					

NOVEMBER

S	M	T	W	T	F	S
			1	2	3	4
5	6	7	8	9	10	11
12	13	14	15	16	17	18
19	20	21	22	23	24	25
26	27	28	29	30		

APRIL

S	M	T	W	T	F	S
						1
2	3	4	5	6	7	8
9	10	11	12	13	14	15
16	17	18	19	20	21	22
23	24	25	26	27	28	29
30						

AUGUST

S	M	T	W	T	F	S
		1	2	3	4	5
6	7	8	9	10	11	12
13	14	15	16	17	18	19
20	21	22	23	24	25	26
27	28	29	30	31		

DECEMBER

S	M	T	W	T	F	S
					1	2
3	4	5	6	7	8	9
10	11	12	13	14	15	16
17	18	19	20	21	22	23
24	25	26	27	28	29	30
31						

FOREIGN EXPRESSIONS

à bientôt (F), so long.

ab initio (L), from the beginning.

à bon marché (F), cheap; a bargain.

ab origine (L), from the origin; from the beginning.

ab ovo (L), from the egg; from the beginning.

ad aperturam (libri) (L), at the opening of the book; wherever the book opens.

ad extremum (L), to the last; extremity.

ad finem (L), to the end; at or near the end.

ad hominem (L), to the man; to one's interests.

ad infinitum (L), to infinity.

ad interim (L), in the meantime.

ad libitum (L), at pleasure; as long as you wish.

ad nauseam (L), to disgust.

ad rem (L), to the purpose; to the point.

à droite (F), to the right.

ad valorem (L), according to the value.

à gauche (F), to the left.

à la carte (F), according to the menu.

à la française (F), after the French style.

à la mode (F), according to the custom or fashion.

al fresco (I), in the open air.

alter ego (L), another self.

alter idem (L), another exactly alike.

amour propre (F), self-love; self-esteem.

ancient régime (F), former order of things.

anno Christi (L),in the year of Christ.

anno Domini (L), in the year of our Lord.

ante meridiem (L), before noon.

à peu près (F), nearly.

à pied (F), on foot.

à point (F), to a point; just in time.

arrière pensée (F), mental reservation.

arrivederci (I), so long.

Artium Magister (L), Master of Arts.

à toute force (F), with all one's might.

à tout prix (F), at any price; at all costs.

au contraire (F), on the contrary.

au courant (F), fully informed; up to date.

au fait (F), well acquainted with; expert.

au fond (F), at bottom; in reality.

auf Wiedersehen (G), till we meet again; so long.

au jour de jour (F), from day to day; from hand to
  mouth.

au naturel (F), in the natural state; nude.

au pis aller (F), at worst.

au revoir (F); till we meet again; so long.

avant-propos (F), preliminary matter; preface.

bête noire (F), black beast; bugaboo.
bêtise (F), stupidity.
bien entendu (F), well understood.
billet d'amour (F), loveletter.
bona fide (L), in good faith.
bona fides (L), good faith.
bon appetit (F), good appetite.
bon jour (F), good day.
bon soir (F), good evening.
bon vivant (F), one who lives well; gourmet.
bon voyage! (F), good journey; good trip.
breveté (F), patented.

cap à pié (F), from head to foot.
carpe diem (L), enjoy, or use, the present day.
carte d'idéntité (F), identity card.
casus belli (L), that which causes or justifies war.
causa sine qua non (L), an indispensable condition.
cause célèbre (F), celebrated case or matter.
caveat emptor (L), let the buyer beware.
cela va sans dire (F), that goes without saying; need-
    less to say.

c'est à dire (F), that is to say.

chacun à son gout (F), everyone to his own taste.

comme ci, comme ca (F), like this, like that; so-so.

comme il faut (F), as it should be.

cordon bleu (F), blue-ribbon.

cordon sanitaire (F), quarantine.

coup de grâce (F), finishing stroke.

coup d'état (F), sudden, decisive blow.

crême de la crême (F), the very best.

cum grano salis (L), with a grain of salt.

de facto (L), actual; actually.

dei gratia (L), by the grace of God.

de jure (L), from the law; by right.

de luxe (F), unusually fine.

de mal en pis (F), from bad to worse.

dénouement (F), outcome; solution.

de novo (L), anew.

Deo volente (L), God willing.

de rigueur (F), indispensable.

de trop (F), too much.

double entendre (F), double meaning; play on words.

dramatis personae (L), characters in the play.

emeritus (L), retired with honor.

en ami (F), as a friend.

en avant (F), forward.

en effet (F), in effect; actually.

en famille (F) with one's family; at home.

enfin (F), in short; at last; finally.

en masse (F), in a mass; in a body.

en passant (F), in passing.

en rapport (F), in harmony; in agreement.

en route (F), on the way.

entourage (F), surroundings; attendants; associates.

entre nous (F), between us.

en vérité (F), in truth.

esprit de corps (F), feeling of unity; morale.

et cetera (L), and the rest.

excerpta (L), extracts.

exempli gratia (L), for example.

ex libris (L), from the books of (used in bookplates).

ex officio (L), by virtue of one's office.

exposé (F), statement; revelation.

ex post facto (L), after the fact; retrospective.

faire suivre (F), please forward.

fait accompli (F), a thing already done.

faux pas (F), false step, misbehavior.

gentilhomme (F), gentleman.

guten Tag (G), good day.

habitué (F), one who is in the habit of frequenting a
  place.

hasta la vista (S), so long.

hoi polloi (Gr), the many; the common people.

homme d'affaires (F), businessman.

homme de lettres (F), man of letters.

hors de combat (F), unable any longer to fight; de-
  feated.

hors d'oeuvre (F), out of course; appetizer, or relish.

içi on parle Français (F), French is spoken here.

idée fixe (F), fixed idea.

id est (L), it is (used in abbreviation, *i.e.*).

impedimenta (L), baggage; luggage.

in camera (L), in the judge's chamber; in secret.

in esse (L), in actuality.

in extremis (L), at the point of death.

infra dignitatem (L), colloquially, *infra dig*, beneath
  one's dignity.

in loco parentis (L), in place of parents.

in medias res (L), in the midst of things.

in memoriam (L), in memory of.

in nomine (L), in the name of.

in perpetuum (L), forever.

in re (L), in the matter of.

in situ (L), in its original situation; in place.

inter alia (L), among other things.

inter nos (L), between us.

in toto (L), entirely.

ipse dixit (L), he himself said it; dogmatic statement.

ipso facto (L), by the fact itself.

ipso jure (L), by the law.

je ne sais quoi (F), I know not what; something or other.

je suis prêt (F), I am ready.

jeu de mots (F), play on words; pun.

jeu d'esprit (F), witticism.

lapsus linguae (L), slip of the tongue.

lares et penates (L), household gods.

l'argent (F), money.

lèse majesté (F), high treason.

le tout ensemble (F), the whole thing.

lettre de créance (F), letter of credit.

lex loci (L), the law of the place.

lingua franca, language used among speakers of other languages; universal language.

ma foi (F), indeed.

magnum opus (L), great work.

maître d'hôtel (F), steward.

mal à propos (F), ill-timed.

mal de mer (F), seasickness.

mal de tête (F), headache.

malentendu (F), misunderstanding; mistake.

mano a mano (S), hand to hand.

modus operandi (L), method of working.

mon ami (F), my friend.

mon cher (F, masc.), my dear.

née (F), born; having as maiden name.

ne plus ultra (L), nothing further; perfection.

n'est çe pas? (F), is it not so?

nicht wahr? (G), is it not so?

n'importe (F), it's no matter.

noblesse oblige (F), obligations of rank.

nolens volens (L), willing or unwilling.

nom de guerre (F), war name; assumed name.

nom de plume (F), pen name.

non compos mentis (L), not of sound mind.

non sequitur (L), it does not follow; incorrect conclusion.

nota bene (L), note well.

nuance (F), shade; subtle variation.

obiter dictum (L), a thing said by the way; passing remark.

oeuvres (F), works.

par avion (F), by airplane; used for airmail.

pardonnez-moi (F), pardon me.

par excellence (F), by way of excellence; superior.

par exemple (F), for example.

pari passu (L), equal; together.

parole d'honneur (F), word of honor.

parvenu (F), person of sudden wealth or position.

passé (F), out of date.

passe-partout (F), masterkey, passport.

pâté de fois gras (F), goose-liver paste.

pâtisserie (F), pastry; pastry shop.

patois (F), dialect.

penchant (F), strong liking.

per annum (L), per year.

per capita (L), by the head; for each person.

per centum (L), by the hundred.

per diem (L), by the day; daily.

per se (L), by, or in, itself.

peu-à-peu (F), little by little; by degrees.

pied-à-terre (F), temporary lodging place.

poco a poco (I), little by little.

poste restante (F), to be left at the post office until called for.

prima facie (L), on first sight; self-evident.

pro bono publico (L), for the good of the public.

pro et contra (L), for and against.

pro forma (L), for the sake of form.

pro rata (L), according to rate; proportionate.

protégé (F), one under the protection of another.

quand même (F), even though; nevertheless.

quid pro quo (L), one thing for another; for value received.

quien sabe? (S), who knows?

quod erat demonstrandum (L), which was to be proved; used in abbreviation, *q.e.d.*

quod vide (L), which see; see that reference; used in abbreviation, *q.v.*

raison d'être (F), reason for existence.

rapprochement (F), act of bringing together.

répondez s'il vous plait (F), reply, if you please; used in abbreviation *RSVP*.

résumé (F), summary or abstract; statement of one's experience.

sang-froid (F), coolness; poise.

sans pareil (F), without equal; superior.

savoir faire (F), knowing how to act; poise.

sic passim (L), so here and there throughout; so everywhere.

s'il vous plait (F), please.

sine die (L), without a day being set.

sine qua non (L), without which, not; indispensable.

sotto voce (I), in an undertone.

status quo (L), the state in which; the existing condition.

sub rosa (L), under the rose; secretly.

sui generis (L), of its own kind; unique.

table d'hôte (F), meal at a fixed price.

tant mieux (F), so much the better.

tant pis (F), so much the worse.

tempus fugit (L), time flies.
terra firma (L), solid earth; a secure foothold.
terra incognita (L), unknown or unexplored region.
tour de force (F), feat of strength or skill.
tout-à-fait (F), wholly, completely.
toute de même (F), all the same.
tout de suite (F), immediately.
tout le monde (F), the whole world.

una voce (L), unanimously.
und so weiter (G), and so forth.

via (L), by way of.
vice versa (L), the order being changed; conversely.
vis-à-vis (F), face to face.
viva voce (L), orally.
voilà tout (F), that's all.

ROMAN NUMERALS

Roman numerals are the system of numbering used by the ancient Romans. The system is based on capital letters, as follows: I (=1), V (=5), X (=10), L (=50), C (=100), D (=500), and M (=1,000). If a letter is followed immediately by one of equal or lesser value, the two values are added: XX=20. If a letter is followed by one of greater value, the first is subtracted from the second: IV=4. A bar over a letter multiplies it by 1,000: $\overline{V}$=5,000; $\overline{M}$=1,000,000.

Arabic Numeral	Roman Numeral	Arabic Numeral	Roman Numeral
1	I	18	XVIII
2	II	19	XIX
3	III	20	XX
4	IV	21	XXI
5	V	22	XXII
6	VI	23	XXIII
7	VII	24	XXIV
8	VIII	25	XXV
9	IX	26	XXVI
10	X	27	XXVII
11	XI	28	VVXIII
12	XII	29	XXIX
13	XIII	30	XXX
14	XIV	40	XL
15	XV	50	L
16	XVI	60	LX
17	XVII	70	LXX

Arabic Numeral	Roman Numeral	Arabic Numeral	Roman Numeral
80	LXXX	800	DCCC
90	XC	900	CM
100	C	1,000	M
200	CC	2,000	MM
300	CCC	5,000	$\bar{V}$
400	CD	10,000	$\bar{X}$
500	D	100,000	$\bar{C}$
600	DC	1,000,000	$\bar{M}$
700	DCC		

WEIGHTS AND MEASURES

Linear Measure

12 inches	=1 foot
3 feet	=1 yard
5 1/2 yards	=1 rod, pole, or perch=16 1/2 feet
40 rods	=1 furlong=220 yards=660 feet
8 furlongs	=1 statute mile=1,760 yards=5,280 feet
3 miles	=1 league=5,280 yards=15,840 feet
6,076.12 feet	=1 nautical, geographical, or sea mile

Area Measure

144 square inches	=1 square foot
9 square feet	=1 square yard=1,296 square inches
30 1/4 sq. yards	=1 square rod=272 1/4 square feet
160 square rods	=1 acre=4,840 square yards=43,560 square feet
640 acres	=1 square mile
1 mile square	=1 section of land
6 miles square	=1 township=36 sections=36 square miles

Cubic Measure

1,728 cubic inches	=1 cubic foot
27 cubic feet	=1 cubic yard

Gunter's or Surveyors' Chain Measure

7.92 inches	=1 link
100 links	=1 chain=4 rods=66 feet
80 chains	=1 statute mile=320 rods=5,280 feet

Liquid Measure

4 gills	=1 pint
2 pints	=1 quart
4 quarts	=1 gallon=8 pints=32 gills
16 fluid ounces	=1 pint

Apothecaries' Fluid Measure

60 minims	=1 fluid dram
8 fluid drams	=1 fluid ounce
16 fluid ounces	=1 pint=128 fluid drams
2 pints	=1 quart=32 fluid ounces= 256 fluid drams
4 quarts	=1 gallon=128 fluid ounces =1,024 fluid drams

Dry Measure

2 pints	=1 quart
8 quarts	=1 peck=16 pints
4 pecks	=1 bushel=32 quarts

Avoirdupois Weight

16 ounces	=1 pound
100 pounds	=1 hundredweight

20 hundredweights =1 ton=2,000 pounds
112 pounds =1 gross or long
hundredweight
20 gross or long
hundredweights =1 gross or long ton=2,240
pounds

Troy Weight

The grain is the same in all three tables of weight (avoirdupois, troy, and apothecaries' weights).

24 grains =1 pennyweight
20 pennyweights =1 ounce troy=480 grains
12 ounces troy =1 pound troy=240
pennyweights= 5,760 grains

Apothecaries' Weight

The grain is the same in all three tables of weight (avoirdupois, troy, and apothecaries' weights).

20 grains =1 scruple
3 scruples =1 dram apothecaries'=60
grains
8 drams
apothecaries' =1 ounce apothecaries'=24
scruples=480 grains
12 ounces
apothecaries' =1 pound apothecaries'=96
drams apothecaries'=288
scruples=5,760 grains

METRIC AND COMMON EQUIVALENTS

Equivalents involving decimals are, in most cases, rounded off to the third decimal place, except when they are exact.

Lengths

1 centimeter	= 0.3937 inch
1 chain (Gunter's or surveyors')	= 66 feet
1 chain (engineers')	= 100 feet
1 fathom	= 6 feet = 1.829 meters
1 foot	= 0.305 meter
1 furlong	= 660 feet
1 hand	= 4 inches
1 inch	= 2.540 centimeters (exactly)
1 kilometer	= 0.621 mile
1 league (land)	= 3 statute mile = 4.828 kilometers
1 meter	= 39.37 inches = 1.094 yards
1 mile (statute)	= 5,280 feet = 1.609 kilometers
1 mile (nautical)	= 1.852 kilometers (exactly) = 1.151 statute miles = 6,076.115 feet
1 yard	= 0.9144 meter (exactly)

Areas

1 acre	= 43,560 square feet = 0.405 hectare
1 hectare	= 10,000 square meters
1 centimeter	= 0.155 square inch

1 square meter = 1.196 square yards
1 square mile = 259.000 hectares

Volume

1 barrel liquid = 31 to 42 gallons
1 barrel dry = 3.281 bushels, struck measure
1 bushel U.S
(struck measure) = 2,150.42 cubic inches (exactly)
1 cord (fire wood) = 128 cubic feet
1 cubic foot = 7.481 gallons = 28.317 cubic decimeters
1 cubic meter = 1.308 cubic yards
1 cubic yard = 0.765 cubic meter
1 board foot = 1 foot long, 1 foot wide, 1 inch thick
1 cup, measuring = 8 fluid ounces = 1/2 liquid pint
1 gallon (U.S.) = 3.785 liters = 0.833 British gallon
1 liter = 1.07 liquid quarts = 0.908 dry quart
1 quart dry (U.S.) = 1.101 liters = 0.969 British quart
1 quart liquid (U. S.) = 0.946 liter = 0.833 British quart
1 tablespoon = 3 teaspoons
1 teaspoon = 1/3 tablespoon

Weights or Masses

1 carat	=200 milligrams
1 gram	=15.432 grains=0.035 ounce avoírdupois
1 hundredweight, gross or long	=112 pounds=50.802 kilograms
1 hundredweight, net or short	=100 pounds=45.359 kilograms
1 kilogram	=2.205 pounds
1 pound avoirdupois	=1.215 troy or apothecaries' pounds=453.59237 grams (exactly)
1 pound troy or apothecaries'	=0.823 avoirdupois pound=373.242 grams
1 ton, gross or long	=2,240 pounds=1.12 net tons (exactly)=1.016 metric tons
1 ton, metric	=2,204.622 pounds=0.984 gross ton=1.102 net tons
1 ton, net or short	=2,000 pounds=0.893 gross ton=0.907 metric ton

CONVERSION OF MEASUREMENTS

Boldface figures are exact; the others are given to seven significant figures.

UNITS OF LENGTH

To Convert from Centimeters:

To	Multiply by
Inches	0.393 700 8
Feet	0.032 808 40
Yards	0.010 936 13
Meters	**0.01**

To Convert from Meters

To	Multiply by
Inches	39.370 08
Feet	3.280 840
Yards	1.093 613
Miles	0.000 621 37
Millimeters	**1,000**
Centimeters	**.100**
Kilometers	**0.001**

To Convert from Inches

To	Multiply by
Feet	0.083 333 33
Yards	0.027 777 78
Centimeters	**2.54**
Meters	**0.025 4**

To Convert from Feet

To	Multiply by
Inches	12
Yards	0.333 333 3
Miles	0.000 189 39
Centimeters	30.48
Meters	0.304 8
Kilometers	0.000 304 8

To Convert from Yards

To	Multiply by
Inches	36
Feet	3
Miles	0.000 568 18
Centimeters	91.44
Meters	0.914 4

To Convert from Miles

To	Multiply by
Inches	63,360
Feet	5,280
Yards	1,760
Centimeters	160,934.4
Meters	1,609.344
Kilometers	1.609 344

UNITS OF MASS

To Convert from Grams

To	*Multiply by*
Grains	15.432 36
Avoirdupois drams	0.564 383 4
Avoirdupois ounces	0.035 273 96
Troy ounces	0.032 150 75
Troy pounds	0.002 679 23
Avoirdupois pound	0.002 204 62
Milligrams	**1,000**
Kilograms	**0.001**

To Convert from Avoirdupois Pounds

To	*Multiply by*
Grains	**7,000**
Avoirdupois drams	**256**
Avoirdupois ounces	**16**
Troy ounces	14.583 33
Troy pounds	1.215 278
Grams	**453.592 37**
Kilograms	**0.453 592 37**
Short hundredweights	**0.01**
Short tons	**0.000 5**
Long tons	**0.000 446 428 6**
Metric tons	**0.000 453 592 37**

To Convert from Kilograms

To	*Multiply by*
Grains	15,432.86

Avoirdupois grams	564.383 4
Avoirdupois ounces	35.273 96
Troy ounces	32.150 75
Troy pounds	2.679 229
Avoirdupois pounds	2.204 623
Grams	1,000
Short hundredweights	0.022 046 23
Short tons	0.001 102 31
Long tons	0.000 984 2
Metric tons	**0.001**

To Convert from Metric Tons

To	*Multiply by*
Avoirdupois pounds	2,204.623
Short hundredweights	22.046 23
Short tons	1.102 311 3
Long tons	0.984 206 5
Kilograms	**1,000**

To Convert from Grains

To	*Multiply by*
Avoirdupois drams	0.036 571 43
Avoirdupois ounces	0.002 285 71
Troy ounces	0.002 083 33
Troy pounds	0.000 173 61
Avoirdupois pounds	0.000 142 86
Milligrams	**64.798 91**
Grams	**0.064 798 91**
Kilograms	**0.000 064 798 91**

To Convert from Troy Ounces

To	Multiply by
Grains	480
Avoirdupois drams	17.554 29
Avoirdupois ounces	1.097 143
Troy pounds	0.083 333 3
Avoirdupois pounds	0.068 571 43
Grams	31.103 476 8

To Convert from Long Tons

To	Multiply by
Avoirdupois ounces	35,840
Avoirdupois pounds	2,240
Short hundredweights	22.4
Short tons	1.12
Kilograms	1,016.046 908 8
Metric tons	1.016 046 908 8

To Convert from Avoirdupois Ounces

To	Multiply by
Grains	437.5
Avoirdupois drams	16
Troy ounces	0.911 458 3
Troy pounds	0.075 954 86
Avoirdupois pounds	0.062 5
Grams	28.349 523 125
Kilograms	0.028 349 523 125

To Convert from Short Hundredweights

To	Multiply by
Avoirdupois pounds	**100**
Short tons	**0.05**
Long tons	0.444 642 86
Kilograms	**45.359 237**
Metric tons	**0.045 359 237**

To Convert from Short Tons

To	Multiply by
Avoirdupois pounds	**2,000**
Short hundredweights	**20**
Long tons	0.892 857 1
Kilograms	**907.184 74**
Metric tons	**0.907 184 74**

To Convert from Troy Pounds

To	Multiply by
Grains	**5,760**
Avoirdupois drams	210.651 4
Avoirdupois ounces	13.165 71
Troy ounces	**12**
Avoirdupois pounds	0.822 857 1
Grams	**373.241 721 6**

UNITS OF VOLUME, LIQUID MEASURE

To Convert from Milliliters

To	Multiply by
Minims	16.230 73

Liquid ounces	0.033 814 02
Gills	0.008 453 5
Liquid pints	0.002 113 4
Liquid quarts	0.001 056 7
Gallons	0.000 264 17
Cubic inches	0.061 023 74
Liters	**0.001**

To Convert from Cubic Meters

To	*Multiply by*
Gallons	264.172 05
Cubic inches	61,023.74
Cubic feet	35.314 67
Liters	**1,000**
Cubic yards	1.307 950 6

To Convert from Liters

To	*Multiply by*
Liquid ounces	33.814 02
Gills	8.453 506
Liquid pints	2.113 376
Liquid quarts	1.056 688
Gallons	0.264 172 05
Cubic inches	61.023 74
Cubic feet	0.035 314 67
Milliliters	**1,000**
Cubic meters	**0.001**
Cubic yards	0.001 307 95

To Convert from Minims

To	Multiply by
Liquid ounces	0.002 083 33
Gills	0.000 520 83
Milliliters	0.061 611 52
Cubic inches	0.003 759 77

To Convert from Liquid Pints

To	Multiply by
Minims	7,680
Liquid ounces	16
Gills	4
Liquid quarts	0.5
Gallons	0.125
Cubic Inches	28.875
Cubic feet	0.016 710 07
Milliliters	473.176 473
Liters	0.473 176 473

To Convert from Gills

To	Multiply by
Minims	1,920
Liquid ounces	4
Liquid pints	0.25
Liquid quarts	0.125
Gallons	0.031 25
Cubic inches	7.218 75
Cubic feet	0.004 177 517
Milliliters	118.294 118 25
Liters	0.118 294 118 25

To Convert from Liquid Ounces

To	Multiply by
Minims	480
Gills	0.25
Liquid pints	0.062 5
Liquid quarts	0.031 25
Gallons	0.007 812 5
Cubic inches	1.804 687 5
Cubic feet	0.001 044 38
Milliliters	29.573 53
Liters	0.029 573 53

To Convert from Cubic Inches

To	Multiply by
Minims	265.974 0
Liquid ounces	0.554 112 6
Gills	0.138 528 1
Liquid pints	0.034 632 03
Liquid quarts	0.017 316 02
Gallons	0.004 329 0
Cubic feet	0.000 578 7
Milliliters	16.387 064
Liters	0.016 387 064
Cubic meters	0.000 016 387 064
Cubic yards	0.000 021 43

To Convert from Liquid Quarts

To	Multiply by
Minims	15,360
Liquid ounces	32

Gills	8
Liquid pints	2
Gallons	0.25
Cubic inches	57.75
Cubic feet	0.033 420 14
Milliliters	946.352 946
Liters	0.946 352 946

To Convert from Cubic Feet

To	Multiply by
Liquid ounces	957.506 5
Gills	239.376 6
Liquid pints	59.844 16
Liquid quarts	29.922 08
Gallons	7.480 519
Cubic inches	1,728
Liters	28.316 846 592
Cubic meters	0.028 316 846 592
Cubic yards	0.037 037 04

To Convert from Cubic Yards

To	Multiply by
Gallons	201 972 0
Cubic inches	46, 656
Cubic feet	27
Liters	746.554 857 984
Cubic meters	0.764 554 857 984

To Convert from Gallons

To	Multiply by
Minims	61,440
Liquid ounces	128
Gills	32
Liquid pints	8
Liquid quarts	4
Cubic inches	231
Cubic feet	0.133 680 6
Milliliters	3,785.411 784
Liters	3.785 411 784
Cubic meters	0.003 785 411 784
Cubic yards	0.004 951 13

UNITS OF VOLUME, DRY MEASURE

To Convert from Liters

To	Multiply by
Dry pints	1.816 166
Dry quarts	0.908 082 98
Pecks	0.113 510 4
Bushels	0.028 377 59
Dekaliters	**0.1**

To Convert from Dekaliters

To	Multiply by
Dry pints	18.161 66
Dry quarts	9.080 829 8
Pecks	1.135 104
Bushels	0.283 775 9
Cubic inches	610.237 4
Cubic feet	0.353 146 7
Liters	**10**

To Convert from Cubic Meters

To	Multiply by
Pecks	113.510 4
Bushels	28.377 59

To Convert from Dry Pints

To	Multiply by
Dry quarts	**0.5**
Pecks	**0.062 5**
Bushels	**0.015 625**

Cubic inches	**33.600 312 5**
Cubic feet	0.019 444 63
Liters	0.550 610 47
Dekaliters	0.055 061 05

To Convert from Dry Quarts

To	*Multiply by*
Dry pints	**2**
Pecks	**0.125**
Bushels	**0.031 25**
Cubic inches	**67.200 625**
Cubic feet	0.038 889 25
Liters	1.101 221
Dekaliters	0.110 122 1

To Convert from Pecks

To	*Multiply by*
Dry pints	**16**
Dry quarts	**8**
Bushels	**0.25**
Cubic inches	**537.605**
Cubic feet	0.311 114
Liters	8.809 767 5
Dekaliters	0.880 976 75
Cubic meters	0.008 809 77
Cubic yards	0.011 522 74

To Convert from Bushels

To	*Multiply by*
Dry pints	**64**

Dry quarts	**32**
Pecks	**4**
Cubic inches	**2,150.42**
Cubic feet	1.244 456
Liters	35.239 07
Dekaliters	3.523 907
Cubic meters	0.035 239 07
Cubic yards	0.046 090 96

To Convert from Cubic Inches

To	*Multiply by*
Dry pints	0.029 761 6
Dry quarts	0.014 880 8
Pecks	0.001 860 10
Bushels	0.000 465 025

To Convert from Cubic Feet

To	*Multiply by*
Dry pints	51.428 09
Dry quarts	25.714 05
Pecks	3.214 256
Bushels	0.803 563 95

To Convert from Cubic Yards

To	*Multiply by*
Pecks	86.784 91
Bushels	21.696 227

UNITS OF AREA

To Convert from Square Centimeters

To	Multiply by
Square inches	0.155 000 3
Square feet	0.001 076 39
Square yards	0.000 119 599
Square meters	**0.0001**

To Convert from Square Meters

To	Multiply by
Square inches	1.550 003
Square feet	10.763 91
Square yards	1.195 990
Acres	0.000 247 105
Square centimeters	**10,000**
Hectares	**0.0001**

To Convert from Hectares

To	Multiply by
Square feet	107,639.1
Square yards	11,959.90
Acres	2.471 054
Square miles	0.003 861 02
Square meters	**10,000**

To Convert from Square Inches

To	Multiply by
Square feet	0.006 944 44
Square yards	0.000 771 605

Square centimeters	**6.451 6**
Square meters	**0.000 645 16**

To Convert from Square Feet

To	*Multiply by*
Square inches	**144**
Square yards	0.111 111 1
Acres	0.000 022 957
Square centimeters	**929.030 4**
Square meters	**0.092 903 04**

To Convert from Square Yards

To	*Multiply by*
Square inches	**1,296**
Square feet	**9**
Acres	0.000 206 611 6
Square miles	0.000 000 322 830 6
Square centimeters	**8,361.273 6**
Square meters	**0.836 127 36**
Hectares	**0.000 083 612 736**

To Convert from Acres

To	*Multiply by*
Square feet	**43,560**
Square yards	**4,840**
Square miles	**0.001 562 5**
Square meters	**4,046.856 422 4**
Hectares	**0.404 685 642 24**

To Convert from Square Miles

To	Multiply by
Square feet	27,878,400
Square yards	3,097,600
Acres	640
Square meters	2,589,988.110 336
Hectares	258.998 811 033 6

INTERNATIONAL COUNTRY AND CITY
TELEPHONE CODES

When direct dialing countries outside the United States, it is necessary to dial 011 and then to use special codes that correspond to our own area codes. The following chart lists those codes for many countries. The boldface number following the country is the country code. The number following the city is the city code. The plus or minus number at the right is the number of hours ahead of or behind Eastern Standard Time. An asterisk indicates that no city code is required in that country.

Algeria* 213	+6
American Samoa* 684	-6
Andorra 33	+6
All points 628	
Argentina 54	+2
Buenos Aires 1	
Australia 61	+15
Melbourne 3	
Sydney 2	
Austria 43	+6
Vienna 1	
Bahrain* 973	+8

Belgium 32   +6
 Brussels 2
 Ghent 91
Belize* 501   -1
Bolivia 591   +1
 Santa Cruz 33
Brazil 55   +2
 Brasilia 61
 Rio de Janeiro 21
Cameroon* 237   +6
Chile 56   +1
 Santiago 2
Colombia 57   0
 Bogota 1
Costa Rica* 506   -1
Cyprus 357   +7
Czechoslovakia 42   +6
 Prague 2
Denmark 45   +6
 Allborg 8
 Copenhagen 1 or 2
Ecuador 593   0
 Cuenca 7
 Quito 2
Egypt 20   +7
 Alexandria 3

Port Said 66

El Salvador* 503   -1

Ethiopia 251   +8

Addis Ababa 1

Fiji* 679   +17

Finland* 679   +17

Helsinki 0

France 33   +6

Marseilles 91

Nice 93

Paris 13, 14, or 18

French   +1

Antilles* 596

French Antilles*   +1

Guadeloupe 590

French Polynesia * 689   -5

Gabon* 241   +6

Germany (former E.Germany) 37   +6

Berlin 2

Germany (former W.Germany) 49   +6

Berlin 30

Frankfurt 69

Munich 89

Greece 30   +7

Athens 1

Rhodes 241

Guam* 671 +15
Guatemala 502 -1
 Guatemala City 2
 Antigua 9
Guyana 592 +2
 Georgetown 2
Haiti 509 0
 Port au Prince 1
Honduras* 504 -1
Hong Kong 852 +13
 Hong Kong 5
 Kowloon 3
Hungary 36 +6
 Budapest 1
Iceland 354 +5
 Akureyri 6
 Hafnarfjorour 1
India 91 +10.5
 Bombay 22
 New Delhi 11
Indonesia 62 +12
 Jakarta 21
Iran 98 +8.5
 Teheran 21
Iraq 964 +8
 Baghdad 1

Ireland 353 +5
 Dublin 1
 Galway 91
Israel 972 +7
 Haifa 4
 Jerusalem 2
 Tel Aviv 3
Italy 39 +6
 Florence 55
 Rome 6
 Venice 41
Ivory Coast* 225 +5
Japan 81 +14
 Tokyo 3
 Yokohama 45
Jordan 962 +7
 Amman 6
Kenya 254 +8
Korea, Republic of 82 +14
 Pusan 51
 Seoul 2
Kuwait* 965 +8
Liberia* 231 +5
Libya 218 +7
 Tripoli 21

New Caledonia* 687 +16
New Zealand 64 +17
 Auckland 9
 Wellington 4
Nicaragua 505 -1
 Managua 2
Nigeria 234 +8
 Lagos 1
Norway 47 +6
 Bergen 5
 Oslo 2
Oman* 968 +9
Pakistan 92 +10
 Islamabad 51
Panama* 507 0
Papua +15
New Guinea* 675
Paraguay 595 +1
 Asuncion 21
Peru 51 0
 Arequipa 54
 Lima 14
Philippines 63 +13
 Manila 2
Poland 48 +6
 Warsaw 22

Portugal 351 +5
 Lisbon 1
Qatar* 974 +9
Romania 40 +7
 Bucharest 0
Saipan* 670 +15
San Marino 39 +6
 All points 541
Saudi Arabia 966 +8
 Riyadh 1
Senegal* 221 +5
Singapore 65 +13
South Africa 27 +7
 Cape Town 21
 Pretoria 12
Spain 34 +6
 Barcelona 3
 Las Palmas
 (Canary Islands) 28
 Madrid 1
 Seville 54
Sri Lanka 94 +10.5
 Kandy 8
Surinam* 597 +15
Sweden 46 +6
 Goteborg 31

Stockholm 8
Switzerland 41 +6
Geneva 22
Lucerne 41
Zurich 1
Taiwan 886 +13
Tainan 6
Taipei 2
Thailand 66 +12
Bangkok 2
Tunisia 216 +6
Tunis 1
Turkey 90 +8
Istanbul 1
Izmir 51
United Arab Emirates 971 +9
Abu Dhabi 2
Dubai 4
United Kingdom 44 +5
Belfast 232
Cardiff 222
Glasgow 41
London 1
Uruguay 598 +2
Mercedes 532
Montevideo 2

Vatican City 39 +6
All points 6
Venezuela 58 +1
Caracas 2
Maracaibo 61
Yemen Arab Republic 967 +8
Amran 2
Yugoslavia 38 +6
Belgrade 11

INDEX

NOTES